Bankroll and Boundaries

David Lawson is a financial wellness strategist and communication expert with a background in behavioral economics and executive coaching. With a passion for helping people master both money and mindset, David specializes in teaching professionals how to set clear boundaries while building wealth and career success.

Bankroll and Boundaries
How to Save Without FOMO

DAVID LAWSON

Published by
Rupa Publications India Pvt. Ltd 2025
7/16, Ansari Road, Daryaganj
New Delhi 110002

Sales centres:
Bengaluru Chennai
Hyderabad Jaipur Kathmandu
Kolkata Mumbai Prayagraj

Copyright © Rupa Publications India Pvt. Ltd 2025

The views and opinions expressed in this book are the author's own and the facts are as reported by him which have been verified to the extent possible, and the publishers are not in any way liable for the same.

All rights reserved.

No part of this publication may be reproduced, transmitted, or stored in a retrieval system, in any form or by any means, electronic, mechanical, photocopying, recording or otherwise, without the prior permission of the publisher.

P-ISBN: 978-93-7003-873-8
E-ISBN: 978-93-7003-102-9

First impression 2025

10 9 8 7 6 5 4 3 2 1

Printed in India

This book is sold subject to the condition that it shall not, by way of trade or otherwise, be lent, resold, hired out, or otherwise circulated, without the publisher's prior consent, in any form of binding or cover other than that in which it is published.

Contents

Part 1: Why Your Bank Account Hates You

1. Champagne Taste, Tap Water Budget — 3
2. Swipe, Tap, Broke — 7
3. The FOMO-Fueled Wallet Drain — 11
4. When 'Treat Yourself' Becomes a Trap — 15
5. Budget Burnout is Real — 19

Part 2: Mindset Shifts for Smarter Spending

6. Soft Life, Smarter Choices — 27
7. Saying No Without Feeling Cheap — 32
8. The Convenience Tax — 37
9. The Emotional Price of Spending — 41
10. Rich Friends, Broke Feelings — 46

Part 3: Everyday Strategies to Save Without Stress

11. The Subscription Purge — 53
12. Impulse-Proof Your Life — 58
13. Traveling Without the Tourist Debt — 63
14. When Fun Costs Too Much — 68
15. The No-Spend Experiment — 72
16. Shopping Smarter, Not Harder — 76

Part 4: Saving Big for Big Dreams

17. The Future You Fund	83
18. Debt Detox Without the Drama	87
19. Emergency Fund, but Make It Fashion	91
20. Investing: No Suit Required	95

Part 5: Long-Term Financial Glow-Up

21. The Side Hustle Safety Net	101
22. Credit Score, but Make it Cute	105
23. Wealth, but Make it Generational	109
24. Your Rich Person Era (It's Coming)	113

Part 6: Living Richer, Spending Smarter

25. The Luxe-for-Less Lifestyle	119
26. Save Without the Sacrifice	123
27. Boundaries, but Make Them Financial	127
28. Spending With Purpose	132

Part 7: Mastering Everyday Money Moves

29. The Lazy Guide to Saving	139
30. Cash Flow, But Make It Sexy	144
31. When Fun Has a Price Tag	149
32. The Financial Audit (Without the Panic)	154
33. The 50/30/20 Rule (But Make It Personal)	159

Part 8: Digital Spending Detox

34. The Algorithm Wants You Broke	167
35. The 3-Click Rule	172
36. Unsubscribing from Broke Culture	177

Part 9: Money & Relationships

37. Love, But Make It Budget-Friendly	185
38. Financial Boundaries in Family Drama	190
39. Friendships & Finances: The Real Talk	195
40. Your Financial Era (And How to Own It)	198

PART 1

Why Your Bank Account Hates You

1

Champagne Taste, Tap Water Budget

IT'S FUNNY HOW EASY IT is to feel rich when you're spending someone else's money—namely, future you. The paycheck lands, and suddenly everything feels within reach. That bottomless brunch? Necessary. Limited-edition sneakers? A non-negotiable. That skincare set with the twelve-step routine? If it's for self-care, it doesn't count, right? You're not alone—living a little (or a lot) feels like a rite of passage these days. After all, what's the point of working hard if you can't enjoy it? But when the good vibes wear off and you check your bank account, reality has a not-so-cute way of slapping you in the face.

At the core of this is a mismatch between the lifestyle you want and the one you can afford. It's not that you're irresponsible—you're just living in a world where indulgence is marketed as self-love and a "treat yourself" mentality feels like basic survival. You work hard, you want nice things, and—if we're being honest—there's a little thrill in knowing you're living above your means. It's a flex until the credit card bill arrives. And even then, it's easy to tell yourself it'll all balance out someday. Someday, when you're earning more. Someday, when life settles down. Someday, when you finally start taking saving seriously.

But here's the truth: that magical "someday" never comes unless you make it happen. The idea that more income will automatically solve your money problems is a lie, and it's one we've all bought into. If that sounds harsh, consider this—how many people do you know who got a raise and suddenly had extra cash lying around? Exactly. More money doesn't fix bad habits; it just makes them more expensive. If you don't know how to handle a $100 impulse buy, a $1,000 paycheck boost won't save you—it'll just raise your impulse-buy budget.

The real problem is that lifestyle creep sneaks up on you. It doesn't happen overnight—it's slow, subtle, and ridiculously easy to justify. One minute you're celebrating a raise with a nicer apartment, and the next, you can't remember how you ever lived without bi-weekly gel manicures and artisanal lattes. Each upgrade feels small—harmless, even—but the costs quietly pile up until you're wondering where all your money went. Spoiler alert: it went to convenience, comfort, and things you convinced yourself were "essentials."

The craziest part? Society practically *expects* you to keep leveling up. The more you earn, the more you're supposed to spend—better wardrobe, better car, better vacations. It's the unspoken rule of adulthood. And if you don't keep up? You feel like you're falling behind. There's a certain pressure to perform wealth, even if your bank balance isn't backing it up. Social media makes it worse—you're constantly bombarded with people living their best, most aesthetically curated lives. They're brunching, jet-setting, and buying whatever fits their mood—and suddenly, you feel like you should be too. What you don't see are the after-hours panic attacks over debt or the savings accounts collecting virtual dust.

But it's not just about appearances. For a lot of us, spending is emotional. You're not just buying a product—you're buying a feeling. A better version of yourself. That dopamine rush you get when you swipe your card isn't random—it's science. Spending triggers your brain's reward system, making you feel good in the moment, even if you regret it later. And when you're stressed, bored, or craving validation, shopping feels like a quick fix. The problem is, the high is temporary—but the financial fallout lasts a whole lot longer.

And here's where it gets messy: emotional spending doesn't always look reckless. It can feel reasonable—like ordering takeout after a tough day or booking a spontaneous weekend trip "because you deserve it." And while you *do* deserve to enjoy your life, the constant splurge cycle eventually catches up. One indulgence leads to another, and before you know it, your bank account is stuck in a permanent state of "I'll figure it out later."

The tricky part is figuring out where to draw the line. In a world where everything is marketed as a need, it's hard to separate the essentials from the extras. That's by design—brands don't just sell products; they sell identities. You're not just buying clothes—you're buying confidence. You're not just paying for convenience—you're buying time. And it's not entirely wrong—sometimes those things genuinely improve your life. The question is, are they worth the trade-off? Because every dollar you spend on instant gratification is a dollar you're not saving for future freedom.

So, how do you break free from the champagne taste cycle without feeling like you're depriving yourself? It's not about cutting out every joy—it's about getting intentional. What actually makes you happy, and what's just a temporary high? You can love the soft life and still make smart money moves—but it starts with recognizing that spending isn't always the flex it seems.

The key is balance—figuring out what luxuries genuinely enhance your life and which ones are just emotional placeholders. You can have the things you love without blowing your savings—if you're willing to be honest with yourself. Because at the end of the day, having a solid bank balance is a bigger flex than any designer bag ever will be. And trust—champagne tastes a whole lot better when your bank account isn't drowning in debt.

2

Swipe, Tap, Broke

IT STARTS INNOCENTLY ENOUGH—A QUICK tap for your morning coffee, a swipe for the rideshare, a casual scroll that turns into a three-item checkout. No cash exchanges hands, no physical reminder of the money leaving your account. It's all sleek, fast, and dangerously easy. Before you know it, a week has passed, and your bank balance looks like it's been through a battle. The culprit? Frictionless payments—the modern magic trick that makes money feel imaginary until you're wondering where it all went.

There's a reason it's so easy to lose track—because when you're swiping, tapping, or clicking "buy now," it doesn't feel like spending real money. It's smooth, seamless, and designed to be painless. You're not counting out cash or watching your wallet shrink—you're just moving your finger. No friction, no second thoughts. And that's exactly how they want it. Every tap is engineered to feel effortless, which means you don't pause long enough to question whether you actually need that third oat milk latte or the "must-have" gadget Instagram convinced you was life-changing.

Here's the thing: your brain is wired to register pain when you part with money—real, physical money. It's called *spending pain*, and it's why handing over a crisp £50 bill feels harder than tapping a card for the same amount. When you pay with cash, you experience a tangible loss—something physical leaves your hands. But with digital payments? That pain signal barely registers. Your brain treats it like a game—numbers on a screen, easily replenished. The less you feel the loss, the more likely you are to spend without thinking. And companies know this.

In fact, frictionless spending is built on psychological hacks that work against you. Every step that's removed—pulling out your card, entering a PIN, counting cash—makes spending easier and faster. Think about how simple it is to tap a card compared to paying with cash. Now, take it further—apps that let you one-click order without even seeing the total, or contactless payments that don't require a signature. It's no accident that spending feels smoother. Every convenience you love is carefully designed to separate you from your money.

And it's not just the big-ticket items. Those small, casual transactions—the £3 coffee here, the £12 streaming subscription there—are the silent assassins. They add up, drip by drip, until your bank account is bleeding out. The term for it? *Micropurchases.* Individually, they feel harmless. Together, they quietly destroy your savings. Because when spending feels so easy, you don't process how much is leaving your account. You tell yourself it's just a few pounds, but the cumulative effect is lethal.

The problem gets worse when everything around you encourages mindless spending. Apps are especially ruthless. In-app purchases, one-click checkouts, and digital wallets are designed to make you spend more without realizing it. And social media? A whole other beast. You're constantly exposed to limited-time drops, "TikTok made me buy it" trends, and influencers who seem to have it all. Every scroll is an invitation to spend—without ever having to touch actual money. And when it's that easy, why would you stop?

Cash, on the other hand, forces you to confront reality. When you hand over physical money, you see and feel the loss. It's harder to ignore the fact that you just dropped £100 on a dinner you barely remember. Studies prove that people spend significantly less when using cash instead of cards. Why? Because cash triggers those pain receptors. You feel the impact immediately—and that feeling stays with you.

But let's be honest—no one's ditching their digital wallets anytime soon. Cash is clunky, and living in a tap-to-pay world isn't exactly optional. So, the question isn't whether to stop using frictionless payments—it's how to outsmart them. And that starts by bringing back the friction. Adding intentional pauses into your spending habits forces your brain to process the transaction as real.

Start by implementing your own "pause points." That means resisting the one-click trap—disable autofill on your payment methods, delete saved cards, and set spending limits where you can. The more steps you add, the more conscious your spending becomes. And when you feel that itch to make an impulse purchase? Try the 24-hour rule—if it still feels like a need tomorrow, go for it. Most of the time, the urgency fades, and your bank account stays intact.

Another game-changer? Track the "invisible" expenses. Those autopilot subscriptions and app payments are sneaky, and they pile up fast. Do a regular subscription audit—cancel what you barely use and question whether you need multiple services doing the same thing. That £7.99 you forgot about every month? That's £96 a year—money that could be working for you instead of disappearing into the void.

And if you really want to feel the weight of your spending,

try going part-cash for high-risk categories—like dining out or entertainment. Having a set amount of physical money for those indulgences makes you more aware of your limits. When it's gone, it's gone. No swiping your way into an overdraft.

The bottom line? Frictionless spending is designed to make you feel like money isn't real—but the consequences are. Bringing back intentionality, no matter how minor, helps you stay in control. Because the last thing you want is to wake up broke, wondering how a few innocent taps and swipes wrecked your financial future.

3

The FOMO-Fueled Wallet Drain

A CASUAL SCROLL—SOMEONE'S SIPPING COCKTAILS on a beach in Mykonos, another friend just posted their "casual" weekend haul of designer bags, and, of course, there's the influencer flaunting a closet that looks like a high-end boutique. Before you know it, you're deep in a rabbit hole of perfectly filtered lifestyles, and suddenly, your perfectly fine life feels...kind of basic. And what do you do when you feel behind? You spend.

FOMO—*Fear of Missing Out*—isn't just a cute internet acronym. It's a powerful emotional trigger, and it's draining your wallet faster than you realize. Social media has turned comparison into a full-time sport, and the game is rigged to make you feel like you're losing. Every post is curated to show the highlight reel—the trips, the outfits, the expensive dinners—and none of the credit card bills that follow. The pressure to keep up is relentless, and whether you're conscious of it or not, your spending is shaped by this constant exposure to other people's "perfect" lives.

Here's the truth: FOMO taps directly into a primal human instinct—our fear of being excluded from the group. Back when survival literally depended on being part of a community, missing out wasn't just inconvenient—it was dangerous. Fast-forward to now, and that instinct hasn't disappeared—it's just evolved. Today, the "group" is your Instagram feed, and being left out means missing the latest brunch spot, viral fashion trend, or weekend getaway. Social media feeds off this ancient fear, weaponizing it against your self-control. Every time you scroll, you're exposed to a world where everyone seems to be living better, spending more, and doing it effortlessly. And the subtle message is clear: if you're not spending, you're not part of the fun.

The most dangerous part? You're not even spending for yourself half the time—you're spending to perform. Social media has turned consumption into a public event. It's not enough to buy the thing—you have to *show* that you bought the thing. And that breeds a vicious cycle: you feel pressured to spend to keep up appearances, even if it means dipping into money you don't really have. And once you start, stopping feels impossible, because there's always someone doing more.

Half of it isn't even authentic. Those "casual" luxury hauls? Sponsored. The jet-set vacations? Credit card debt wrapped in a filter. Social media isn't reality—it's a carefully crafted illusion designed to provoke envy. And when you're chasing an illusion, you're setting yourself up to lose. The question is, how do you break free from the spending spiral without feeling like you're missing out on everything?

It starts with recognizing the emotional manipulation at play. FOMO spending isn't really about the stuff—it's about the feelings the stuff promises. That £300 bag isn't just a bag—it's a ticket to belonging, a badge that says, "I'm part of the club." But here's the catch: the thrill of the purchase fades fast. Studies show that experiences, not things, provide lasting happiness—but FOMO tricks you into craving the temporary high of new stuff. And once the buzz wears off? You're left with a lighter bank account and the same hollow feeling that sent you shopping in the first place.

So, how do you resist the trap without retreating to a cave

and deleting all your social media? By shifting from *reactive* spending to *intentional* spending. That means recognizing when your spending is driven by external pressure versus internal desire. Ask yourself: *Would I want this if no one else knew I had it?* If the answer is no, you're probably buying for the 'gram—not for yourself.

Another game-changer? Curate your digital environment. Social media isn't just entertainment—it's a constant stream of influence. If your feed is flooded with people whose lifestyle pressures you to overspend, it's time for a detox. Unfollow accounts that trigger unnecessary comparison and replace them with content that reflects your actual goals. You control what you consume—so make sure it's not pushing you to spend money you don't have.

And here's the thing—real financial freedom isn't about *not spending*. It's about choosing *what* to spend on and *why*. You don't need to say no to everything—you just need to decide what actually adds value to your life. Maybe it's that one trip you've dreamed of for years. Maybe it's a wardrobe investment that makes you feel like a boss every time you wear it. Whatever it is, spend intentionally. The difference between FOMO spending and intentional spending? FOMO spending leaves you chasing the next thing. Intentional spending leaves you satisfied.

One practical trick to curb FOMO-fueled spending is to build your own "Joy List." Instead of reacting to every shiny thing social media throws at you, make a running list of purchases or experiences that genuinely bring you happiness. When the impulse to spend hits, check your list. If it's not on there, pause. Most FOMO purchases are fueled by fleeting emotions—letting the urge sit for 24 hours can stop you from making choices you'll regret.

And don't underestimate the power of reframing. You're not "missing out" by saving money—you're buying something far more valuable: freedom. Every time you resist an impulse purchase, you're paying yourself instead of paying for someone else's fantasy. That's the kind of flex no one talks about—but it's the one that actually matters.

At the end of the day, FOMO spending is a game—and the house always wins. Brands, influencers, and algorithms are designed to make you feel like you're falling behind unless you buy in. But here's the truth they don't tell you: the people who are truly thriving? They're not drowning in stuff—they're owning their choices. And the real flex? Building a life so good, you don't need anyone else's approval to enjoy it.

4

When 'Treat Yourself' Becomes a Trap

SELF-LOVE SHOULDN'T COME WITH A credit card bill. But somewhere between "you only live once" and the rise of self-care culture, spending became the ultimate coping mechanism. A rough day? Buy the shoes. Hit a goal? Splurge on a fancy dinner. Existing in this economy? You deserve a weekend getaway.

And listen—treating yourself isn't the problem. It's the *constant* treating that sneaks up on you. Those little indulgences—harmless on their own—pile up fast. A latte here, a random online haul there, and suddenly you're wondering why your bank balance looks like it needs life support. What started as a harmless reward turns into a reflex. Feel bad? Spend. Feel good? Spend. And like clockwork, you're stuck in a cycle where every emotion has a price tag.

The scariest part? It doesn't even feel reckless. The phrase *"I deserve it"* makes every purchase feel like an act of self-care instead of what it really is—emotional spending in disguise. It's easy to justify, especially when everyone else seems to be living their best, most luxurious lives. But behind those perfectly curated Instagram stories is a truth no one's bragging about: the overdraft fees, the mounting credit card debt, and the gut-punching realization that no amount of spontaneous spending will ever fix burnout or boredom.

The Psychology of "I Deserve It"

When you buy something as a "reward," it doesn't just feel good—it rewires your brain. Every time you tap that card, your brain releases a rush of dopamine—the feel-good chemical tied to pleasure and motivation. It's the same high that comes from falling in love or hitting a jackpot. And just like any thrill, you crave it again and again.

The problem? Dopamine isn't about satisfaction—it's about the chase. Once the buzz fades, you're left with the same feelings that drove you to spend in the first place. So, you repeat the process: chase, spend, regret, repeat. It's a financial hamster wheel disguised as self-love.

Worse, the spending trap doesn't just hit your wallet—it messes with your sense of worth. You start associating comfort and happiness with buying things instead of, well, actual fulfillment. And when money's tight? The spending feels even more justified. It's easy to convince yourself that a new outfit or a $20 DoorDash order is a small price for sanity when the world feels chaotic.

When Does "Treating Yourself" Go Too Far?

The line between mindful indulgence and financial sabotage is thin—but it's there if you know where to look. Ask yourself:

> *Is this spending intentional, or is it an emotional reflex?*
> *Would I still want this if no one else could see it?*
> *Is this purchase helping or distracting me from something deeper?*

Real self-care doesn't mean numbing yourself with impulse buys. It means doing the things that make your life *better*—not just easier. And spoiler alert: building a life you love doesn't always come wrapped in fancy packaging.

The truth is, you can spoil yourself without wrecking your financial future—but it takes intention. If every emotional trigger leads you to swipe your card, you're not treating yourself—you're avoiding yourself.

The Art of Smart Indulgence

Here's the thing: you shouldn't have to choose between living your life and building your bank account. The goal isn't to cut out fun—it's to stop confusing mindless spending with genuine joy.

Instead of grabbing every shiny thing the second you want it, shift to planned indulgence. Create a "treat fund"—a guilt-free stash specifically for things that make you happy. Whether it's monthly spa days or that designer bag you've been eyeing, having a separate pool for luxuries keeps you from dipping into your savings.

If you want something, wait 24 hours. For bigger purchases? Wait 30 days. Urgency fades fast when it's not tied to emotion. You'll be surprised how often the must-have impulse dies when you give yourself room to think.

Flip the script—tie your splurges to actual progress. Hit a savings milestone? Treat yourself. Finished a tough project? Go celebrate. Linking indulgence to achievements makes it feel deserved—because it is.

Not all indulgence requires a checkout line. Sleep in. Take a mental health day. Binge your favourite show in your comfiest sweats. The most luxurious things are often the ones that don't cost a dime.

Freedom > Fleeting Thrills

The ultimate treat? Knowing you're in control. Not of every spending urge—but of your *choices*. When you stop chasing temporary highs, you free yourself to enjoy life on your terms—without the lingering anxiety of wondering if you'll make it to payday.

So, the next time the urge to "treat yourself" strikes, ask yourself this: *Is this making my life better—or just easier for now?* Because the best indulgence isn't something you buy—it's the freedom to live a life that doesn't need an escape.

5

Budget Burnout is Real

THERE'S A CERTAIN KIND OF exhaustion that hits when you're trying to "be good" with money. You start strong—color-coded spreadsheets, a fresh budgeting app on your phone, and a resolution to track every coffee swipe like it's a national emergency. For the first week or two, you're unstoppable. You even say no to that second oat milk latte because, apparently, that's what "fiscally responsible" people do.

But then life happens. The group chat blows up with plans for an impromptu weekend getaway, and you're faced with a choice: stick to the budget and feel like a social hermit, or tap "yes" and figure it out later. Spoiler alert—most people choose the latter. And who could blame you? The problem isn't that you're bad with money. The problem is that most budgets are about as realistic as those "clean girl aesthetic" routines where someone wakes up at 5 AM to journal and sip matcha in a sunlit kitchen.

Budget burnout is what happens when you try to fit your messy, spontaneous, joy-seeking life into a box that wasn't designed for it. And if you're feeling exhausted by your own finances, you're not broken. Your budget is.

The reality is, traditional budgeting methods are a relic from a time when people paid for things with paper checks and cash envelopes. Back then, you couldn't impulse-buy a designer bag at midnight with a single swipe. But today? Your bank account is under constant attack—from one-click shopping, tap-to-pay technology, and apps designed to make spending feel as frictionless as possible. Pair that with the pressure to live your "best life" on social media, and no wonder your perfectly planned budget never lasts.

Why Traditional Budgets Are Basically Financial Diets (And Just as Doomed)

If you've ever tried to cut carbs, you already know how this works. You start by swearing off bread, pasta, and everything fun. For a while, it feels manageable. But eventually, you crack. And when you do, it's not a nibble—it's a full-blown carb bender with zero regrets until the guilt kicks in. Budgeting works the same way. The more you restrict yourself, the more likely you are to rebel.

That's because most budgets operate on an outdated premise: if you just track your spending and have enough willpower, everything will fall into place. But here's the catch—willpower is a finite resource, and the modern world is engineered to drain it. Every notification, every limited-time offer, every "this could be you" Instagram post chips away at your resolve.

So, what happens next? You blow the budget. And instead of reassessing the plan, you blame yourself. But the issue isn't that you lack self-control—it's that your budget was never built to accommodate real life.

The Mental Load of Budgeting (And Why It's Exhausting)

Here's the thing no one tells you: budgeting is mentally exhausting because it turns every purchase into a moral decision. You start questioning everything—Is this coffee worth it? Should I cancel my streaming subscription? Do I really need those concert tickets? And while that might sound responsible, it's also draining.

When every dollar feels like a test of your financial virtue, spending becomes a source of guilt instead of empowerment. And the more you agonize over every purchase, the easier it is to fall into the "screw it" mentality. Because if you're already over budget, why not go all the way?

This mental tug-of-war isn't just tiring—it's unsustainable. And that's the real reason most people abandon their budgets. It's not because you're weak—it's because no one thrives under a system that treats joy like a luxury you can't afford.

Ditch the Budget—Build a Spending Plan Instead

If budgeting feels like punishment, here's a radical idea: stop doing it. Ditch the guilt-ridden spreadsheets and switch to a spending plan that actually works with how you live. Because the truth is, you don't need a financial boot camp—you need a system that respects your life *and* your bank account.

A spending plan isn't about deprivation. It's about intention. It shifts the focus from "what can I cut?" to "what do I value?"—and that change makes all the difference. Instead of tracking every penny, you're assigning your money to categories that reflect what matters to you.

Think of it like this: you're not cutting out joy—you're curating it. Your spending plan is less about saying no and more about deciding where to say hell yes.

Here's how you start:

1. **Prioritize Essentials.** This is your "life stuff"—rent, groceries, transportation. These expenses keep the lights on and your stomach full. Non-negotiable.
2. **Pay Future You First.** This is the money you save or

invest—because present-you is great, but future-you deserves a shot at financial freedom.
3. **Fun with Boundaries.** This is your permission slip to enjoy life without blowing your goals. It's for brunch, vacations, and yes, that overpriced artisanal candle.
4. **The Chaos Fund.** Life is unpredictable—your spending plan should reflect that. This cushion is for when things go sideways, so you're prepared without panic.

This isn't a rigid system. It's flexible enough to accommodate life's twists while keeping you financially grounded. And best of all? It removes the shame spiral from spending.

Why Flexibility is the Secret to Consistency

Here's a secret that financial "experts" rarely mention: the best plan is the one you can stick to. Rigid budgets might work in theory, but flexible spending plans work in real life.

When you give yourself permission to spend on what you love, you eliminate the scarcity mindset that leads to binge-spending. You're no longer white-knuckling through life waiting for the moment you snap. Instead, you're making intentional choices that honor your present *and* your future.

It's also about recognizing that money is meant to be used—not hoarded. There's nothing noble about sitting on a mountain of cash while denying yourself experiences that bring you joy. A good spending plan balances both—so you can enjoy today while building the life you want tomorrow.

The ultimate flex isn't having a massive savings account—it's having a financial system that works on your terms. And that means leaving behind the shame-driven, scarcity-obsessed budgeting models that burn you out.

A spending plan, on the other hand, is built for the messy,

joyful, unpredictable reality of modern life. It gives you the freedom to say yes to what matters, no to what doesn't, and enough breathing room to enjoy the ride.

So, if you're tired of feeling like you're failing at budgeting, maybe it's time to question the system—not yourself. Because the real goal isn't to spend less—it's to spend smarter in a way that makes your whole life richer.

And that? That's the kind of financial freedom no spreadsheet can give you.

PART 2

Mindset Shifts for Smarter Spending

6

Soft Life, Smarter Choices

THERE'S A REASON THE "SOFT LIFE" aesthetic has taken over your feeds. It's all cashmere throws, organic brunches, and stress-free living. It's an escape from hustle culture—a middle finger to the grind. And honestly? Who doesn't want a life that feels like a warm hug? But here's the catch: the soft life can get *real* expensive, *real* fast. The line between treating yourself and financially sabotaging yourself is thin—and easy to blur when you're just one click away from a dopamine-fueled shopping spree.

But let's get one thing straight—enjoying nice things doesn't make you irresponsible. The narrative that luxury is only for the wealthy? Outdated. You don't have to choose between enjoying your life and being financially smart. What you *do* need is a mindset shift that lets you indulge without draining your bank account.

Living soft doesn't mean living recklessly—it means living intentionally. And the real flex? Knowing how to prioritize what matters without sacrificing your financial future. So, how do you pull that off? It's less about cutting out the fancy coffee and more about defining your *non-negotiables*.

Luxury Isn't the Enemy—Mindless Spending Is

The soft life gets a bad reputation because people assume it's all impulse buys and frivolous spending. But the truth? It's not about how much something costs—it's about how much value it adds to your life. There's a difference between buying a silk robe you wear daily and one that sits in your closet gathering dust. One elevates your daily routine. The other is just... clutter.

Here's where people mess up: They chase the *idea* of luxury instead of what actually feels luxurious to them. That's how you end up spending money on things that look good in theory but don't really improve your life. The key is knowing what brings *you* joy—not what Instagram says should.

That $8 latte might be your morning ritual, the thing that starts your day on the right foot. If it adds value, it's worth it. But if you're only buying it because everyone else is posting their perfectly frothed oat milk art—pause. Is it really making your life better, or are you paying for an aesthetic?

This is where intentionality comes in. Soft living isn't about saying yes to everything—it's about curating the things that bring real joy. And when you're clear on your non-negotiables, you can spend freely on what matters *and* keep your financial goals in check.

Curating Your "Non-Negotiables"

Think of your non-negotiables as your financial love language. These are the things that make your life feel good—the things you're willing to spend on without guilt. Maybe it's bi-weekly facials because they help you unwind. Maybe it's premium groceries because you value nourishing yourself well. Whatever they are, owning them means you're not wasting money—you're investing in your quality of life.

The mistake people make is trying to do *everything*. They want designer bags *and* spontaneous trips *and* a new skincare line every month. But soft living doesn't mean having it all—it means choosing what actually matters to *you*.

Here's how to figure out your non-negotiables:

1. **Ask Yourself What Feels Essential.** What are the things that make your life feel elevated? Is it the gym membership that keeps you sane? High-end beauty products that make your skin glow? Identify the things that feel like an extension of your best self.
2. **Separate Joy from FOMO.** Are you spending because you genuinely enjoy it, or because everyone else is doing it? If it doesn't light you up, it's not a non-negotiable—it's just noise.
3. **Be Honest About Frequency.** Not everything has to be a weekly indulgence. Maybe monthly massages are sustainable, but weekly shopping sprees aren't. Define what feels good without overstretching your finances.

When you lock in your non-negotiables, spending becomes clearer. You're not saying no to everything—you're just saying yes to the right things.

The Art of Soft Living Without Going Broke

The biggest myth about living soft? That you have to spend recklessly to do it. In reality, it's not about the price tag—it's about the *experience*. The difference between blowing your budget and building a beautiful life is intention.

Start by adopting a "quality over quantity" mindset. Instead of buying five trendy fast-fashion pieces, invest in one timeless item that feels luxurious every time you wear it. Instead of spending mindlessly on every social invite, choose experiences that align with your values—like a weekend getaway with your closest friends over a dozen random nights out.

And don't underestimate the power of small luxuries. A $20 candle you light every evening can feel more indulgent than a splurge that leaves your bank account crying. It's not about having everything—it's about savoring the things you choose.

Soft living is also about **slowing down**. We live in a world that tells us to want more, buy more, do more—but what if you let yourself enjoy what you already have? Luxuries feel richer when you're not rushing through them. Take time to actually enjoy that fancy coffee. Relish the quiet of a spa night at home. Let yourself *feel* the softness—you don't need to spend endlessly to get it.

Balancing Soft Living with Financial Goals

Here's the truth no one talks about: You can live soft and still be financially smart. You don't have to choose between your now and your future—you just need balance.

The key is making your spending intentional while still leaving room for your financial goals. One doesn't have to cancel out the other. Think of it like a wardrobe—your savings and investments are the timeless essentials, and your indulgences are the statement pieces. Both matter. Both have a place.

So how do you strike that balance?

Create a "Soft Life" Fund. Set aside money specifically for the things that bring you joy. This isn't "extra" spending—it's a built-in part of your financial plan.

Be Selective, Not Restrictive. Don't cut yourself off from joy—but be intentional. Prioritize what truly enriches your life, and let go of what doesn't.

Treat Soft Living as an Investment. You're not "wasting" money on things that make life better. A life that feels good is worth investing in—but do it wisely.

Soft living doesn't mean financial recklessness. It means you get to define luxury on your terms—and when you're clear on what matters, you can have both the plush life and the padded bank account.

And the best part? You'll never feel like you're missing out—because when you choose what matters most, everything else fades into the background.

7

Saying No Without Feeling Cheap

THERE'S A SPECIAL KIND OF panic that hits when your group chat drops the "weekend getaway" plan. The idea sounds dreamy—rooftop brunches, spa sessions, and an aesthetically pleasing Airbnb—but your bank account? Not so enthusiastic. Saying no to plans without feeling like the broke friend isn't easy, especially when it feels like everyone else is living their best, most expensive life. And in a culture where social currency often feels as valuable as actual currency, opting out can make you feel like you're falling behind.

But here's the truth: setting financial boundaries doesn't make you stingy—it makes you smart. Saying no isn't about being cheap or missing out. It's about protecting your peace (and your paycheck) while still showing up for the moments that matter. The real glow-up? Knowing how to say no without the guilt trip. Because you don't need to drain your savings to maintain your social life—you just need a better strategy.

The first myth to ditch? The idea that you're obligated to say yes to every invite. Social pressure might tell you otherwise, but no one's keeping a tally of how many times you say yes or no. And the people worth keeping around? They care about *you*, not how much you spend to be in their company. Still, navigating these conversations can feel like tiptoeing through a financial minefield. So how do you decline without the awkwardness or feeling like a buzzkill?

Normalizing the No

Let's be honest—no one likes feeling left out. There's a subtle panic that bubbles up when you turn down plans, as if missing that one dinner means you'll become a distant memory. But here's the kicker: most people aren't as obsessed with your absence as you think. While you're spiraling about seeming cheap, everyone else is deciding whether to order the pasta or the steak.

Saying no without guilt starts with realizing your presence isn't defined by how much money you spend. You can be the friend who skips the weekend trip but shows up when it really counts. And when you're upfront about your priorities, you set the tone for how people treat your boundaries. The key is being honest without oversharing—no one needs a full TED Talk on your monthly budget breakdown.

Instead of over-explaining, keep it simple. You don't need an elaborate excuse, and you're not required to justify your decision. A direct, confident "I'm sitting this one out, but let's catch up soon" does the trick. The less awkward *you* make it, the less awkward it becomes for everyone else.

And here's the real flex: when you're secure in your "no," people respect it. If someone makes you feel bad for protecting your finances, that says more about them than it does about you. The people who matter won't question your boundaries—they'll honor them.

When Friends Overspend

We all have *that* friend. The one who suggests the bougiest restaurants, spontaneous weekend trips, and boutique fitness classes that cost more than your monthly Wi-Fi bill. And while their energy is unmatched, keeping up with them can be financially exhausting. The tricky part? Telling them you can't match their spending without feeling like the group cheapskate.

The secret is shifting the narrative. Instead of framing it as "I can't afford it," position it as a choice you're making. There's a world of difference between "I'm broke" and "I'm focusing on other financial goals right now." The first makes you sound helpless—the second makes you sound intentional.

When a friend's spending pace doesn't align with yours, don't ghost them—pivot the plans. Suggest alternatives that feel fun but aren't financially draining. If your bestie wants to hit up a pricey rooftop bar, offer to meet for a coffee date instead. It's not about rejecting the friendship—it's about finding a middle ground where both your wallets can breathe.

And if they push back? Stay firm without apologizing. You don't owe anyone a financial performance. A simple "I'm keeping things low-key right now" is enough. The right people won't make you feel bad about prioritizing your bank account.

The "Let's Split the Bill" Struggle

Few things spark tension faster than a group dinner and the inevitable "let's just split it evenly" moment. It's all fun and games until you're paying for someone else's imported truffle risotto while you nibbled on fries.

The fear of being "that person" who asks to pay only for what they ordered is real—but so is watching your money disappear over other people's indulgences. The solution? Address it before the check arrives.

When the waiter comes around, casually mention you'll be paying separately. No drama, no awkwardness—just a quick, polite heads-up. Most people won't bat an eye. If it feels too formal, add a bit of lightness: "I'm keeping it simple today, so I'll just grab my tab!" Done and dusted.

If the group still pushes for an even split, don't be afraid to speak up. You're not a villain for wanting fairness. A breezy "I'll just cover my share if that's cool!" keeps things friendly while protecting your finances. And if you're close with the group, be honest: "I'm watching my spending right now, so I'll pay for what I had." No need to apologize for being smart with your money.

The people who value you won't judge you for protecting your financial peace. And if they do? Maybe it's time to rethink who you're breaking bread with.

Scripts That Save Your Sanity (and Wallet)

Knowing what to say makes all the difference. When you have a few go-to responses ready, saying no becomes easier—and less stressful. Here are a few scripts to keep in your back pocket:

For Expensive Plans:
"I'm sitting this one out, but I'm down for a catch-up soon!"
For Group Splits:
"I'll just cover my part—I'm keeping it simple today!"
For Pricey Friends:
"I'm keeping things low-key right now, but I'd love to hang in a way that's easier on my budget."
For Last-Minute Invites:
"That sounds amazing, but it's not in my budget right now. Rain check?"

These lines are simple, direct, and most importantly—guilt-free. You're not making excuses. You're making choices.

And here's the thing: setting financial boundaries isn't a sign of lack—it's a sign of confidence. It says you know your worth, and you're not willing to spend recklessly just to fit in.

So, the next time you're faced with an invite that doesn't align with your budget, remember—you're not missing out. You're choosing what matters most. And that? That's a power move.

8

The Convenience Tax

MODERN LIFE IS A BUFFET of conveniences, and we're all feasting. One-click orders, same-day delivery, and a subscription service for everything you can imagine—convenience is the ultimate luxury. And why not? In a world that's always rushing, who wouldn't pay a little extra to make life easier? The only catch? That "little extra" adds up faster than you realize. Convenience doesn't just save time—it quietly drains your bank account.

Think about the last time you were too tired to cook. That quick delivery order? An extra £5 in fees alone. The streaming service you barely use but can't quite bring yourself to cancel? Another £12 a month. The express shipping you didn't *need*, but hey—it was only £3. Harmless, right? Except those small, invisible charges pile up into something far more serious: a slow leak in your financial foundation.

But here's the tricky part—convenience isn't always the enemy. Sometimes it buys back your time, energy, and sanity in ways that feel priceless. The goal isn't to cut every corner and live like a budgeting monk. It's about recognizing when you're paying for ease at the expense of your long-term financial health—and when it's genuinely worth it. Because if you're not careful, convenience can quietly become the most expensive habit you never meant to form.

The True Cost of Convenience

The genius of convenience spending is that it rarely feels expensive in the moment. A delivery fee here, a subscription there—each one is small enough to feel like no big deal. But those "no big deals" become a major deal when they silently siphon hundreds from your account every year.

Take food delivery. Ordering in on a busy night feels like a harmless indulgence—until you realize you're spending 30-40% more on the same meal than you would by picking it up yourself. And it's not just the obvious fees—the service charges, tips, and "small cart" penalties sneak in like silent thieves.

Then there are the subscriptions. Gym memberships, streaming platforms, meal kits—you name it. They're designed to be out of sight, out of mind. Automated payments keep you locked in while you forget you're even paying. A £10 subscription doesn't feel like much until you realize you've had five of them quietly draining your account for months.

And let's not forget the premium we pay for urgency. Express shipping. Same-day delivery. Convenience stores. They capitalize on impatience, charging you a premium just because you want it *now*. And because it's framed as a small fee—£2 here, £5 there—it's easy to brush off. But those little "time savers" snowball into a very real financial burden.

The Sneaky Upsell Game

What makes convenience spending so dangerous is how seamless it feels. Brands have mastered the art of making you spend more without you realizing it. It's not just about what you buy—it's how easily they make you say "yes."

The classic trap? The convenience markup. This isn't just about higher prices—it's the subtle ways companies nudge you to spend more. The "recommended add-ons" when you place an order. The "small fee" for expedited shipping. The fact that one-click purchases eliminate the mental pause you'd take in a store.

Even the design of apps and checkout pages plays into it. Delivery services don't just offer food—they sell ease. Grocery apps suggest pricier items because they know you'll add them to save time. And the psychology of "just one more click" makes it easier to pay a little extra rather than rethink your purchase.

And let's be honest—convenience feels good. There's a dopamine hit in knowing something will arrive quickly or that you don't need to leave the house. It's immediate gratification disguised as necessity. And companies bank on the fact that you won't notice the cost until it's too late.

When Convenience is Worth It

Not all convenience spending is bad. Sometimes, it's a game-changer. Paying for ease is smart when it genuinely adds value to your life—saving time, reducing stress, or improving your well-being. The trick is knowing where to draw the line.

If you're buying back time that allows you to earn more or take care of yourself, the extra cost can be worth it. For instance, a meal delivery service that stops you from stress-eating takeout five nights a week might actually *save* you money. Likewise, a laundry service could be a lifesaver if it frees up hours you'd otherwise lose.

But the difference lies in whether it's a conscious decision or a mindless habit. If you're leaning on convenience as a crutch—ordering delivery because you didn't plan meals, paying rush fees because you forgot a deadline—it's not saving you anything. It's just costing you more.

A helpful filter: ask yourself, "Is this expense making my life meaningfully easier, or am I just avoiding a minor inconvenience?" If it's the latter, chances are, you're paying more than it's worth.

Convenience itself isn't the villain—it's the mindless consumption of it that drains your bank account. To take control, you don't need to cut out every little luxury. You just need to become a more intentional spender.

Take stock of every recurring charge hitting your account. If you're not actively using a service—or if it's something you can live without—it's time to cancel. Even if it's just £5 a month, that's £60 a year you could reclaim. Next time you're about to pay for convenience, take a mental beat. Do you *need* that express shipping, or can you wait a couple of days? Could you grab that coffee on your way home instead of paying for delivery? Small shifts in behaviour add up.

If you can't imagine cutting a subscription entirely, see if you can bundle services for a discount. Many platforms offer combined packages—like music and video streaming—at a lower rate. Rather than eliminating ease, give yourself a limit. Set a monthly allowance for convenience spending—whether it's delivery, ride-shares, or premium services—and stick to it. This lets you enjoy ease without overspending.

Some conveniences are worth every penny—others aren't. Decide which ones genuinely add value to your life and cut the rest. If a house-cleaning service gives you your weekends back, keep it. If you're paying for three different video streaming services but only use one? Let the others go.

Convenience is seductive—there's no denying that. But when you start to separate the helpful from the habitual, you take back control. Your time is valuable—but so is your financial peace. And nothing feels better than knowing you're spending on purpose, not just out of habit.

9

The Emotional Price of Spending

NO ONE PULLS OUT THEIR credit card in a vacuum. Behind every purchase—whether it's a £5 latte or a splurge-worthy designer bag—there's a feeling. A little rush of excitement, a fleeting sense of comfort, maybe even a temporary escape. The truth is, spending is rarely just about the object itself. More often than not, it's about how we *feel* when we buy it.

You don't wake up one day and think, *Today, I'll emotionally sabotage my bank account*. It's subtler than that. A tough week melts into an impulsive "treat yourself" moment. A wave of boredom becomes an online shopping spiral at midnight. Sadness? There's a cart full of things promising to cheer you up. But the emotional price tag attached to those quick fixes is a lot higher than it seems—because when you're spending to soothe, you're usually not spending wisely.

Understanding the emotional undercurrent of your purchases isn't about shaming yourself for every indulgence. It's about recognizing when your feelings are in the driver's seat and learning how to take the wheel back. Because while a shopping spree might lift your mood for a moment, the financial anxiety that follows isn't worth the temporary high.

Feelings vs. Finances

Emotions are messy—and money, despite all its neat numbers, is just as tangled. The intersection of the two is where things get interesting (and expensive). Studies show that most financial decisions aren't purely logical. Your mood, your stress levels, even your sense of identity—all of it influences how you spend.

Take retail therapy. It's not just a catchy phrase—it's a real psychological coping mechanism. When you shop, your brain releases dopamine, the same feel-good neurotransmitter linked to pleasure and reward. That little dopamine hit makes you feel temporarily happier, more in control, even a bit invincible. But the buzz doesn't last. Once it fades, you're left with the same feelings you were trying to avoid—plus a dent in your bank account.

And it's not just sadness or stress that triggers spending. Happiness can be just as dangerous. Ever noticed how easy it is to overspend when you're celebrating? Whether it's a promotion or a friend's engagement, positive emotions lower your spending inhibitions. When you feel good, you're more likely to justify indulgences because, well, *you deserve it*. But emotional spending doesn't just drain your wallet—it creates a cycle that's hard to break.

The Mood-Based Shopping Trap

Emotional spending isn't always loud and obvious. Sometimes, it's a quiet hum in the background of your daily routine—an autopilot response to feelings you may not even notice. The trickiest part? Different emotions trigger different spending patterns, and knowing your emotional triggers is the first step to breaking free.

Stress tends to push us toward quick, convenient fixes.

That's why a rough day often leads to impulse food delivery or a spontaneous shopping cart full of things you never planned to buy. Sadness? It's the emotional sweet spot for comfort purchases—soft blankets, candles, or anything promising to fill an emotional gap.

Loneliness has its own spending profile. When you're craving connection, you might splurge on experiences, beauty products, or clothes that promise to "reinvent" you. And boredom? That's the silent budget killer. Scrolling through shopping apps becomes a mindless habit, and without realizing it, you're spending simply to entertain yourself.

The most dangerous spending trigger, though, might be comparison. Social media fuels an endless highlight reel of vacations, designer hauls, and "must-have" products. Seeing other people's perfectly curated lives can spark a sense of inadequacy—or a need to "keep up." Suddenly, you're buying things you never wanted until you saw someone else had them.

The Dopamine Loop of Retail Therapy

Here's the thing about emotional spending—it *works*. At least, for a little while. The anticipation of a package arriving, the thrill of an unplanned splurge, the sense of newness—it's a potent emotional cocktail. But once the novelty fades, the feelings you were trying to outrun come rushing back. Worse, there's often a fresh layer of guilt or anxiety about the money you just spent.

It's a cycle: Feel something uncomfortable. Spend to soothe it. Feel better temporarily. Then, crash. And because the relief is so fleeting, you're tempted to chase the next high. This is how emotional spending becomes a habit—your brain starts to associate shopping with relief, and soon, it becomes a reflex.

The sneakiest part? This loop is designed to keep you hooked. Retailers know exactly how to keep your dopamine levels spiking.

Limited-time offers, flash sales, and the thrill of "exclusive" products play directly into your brain's reward system. And in the digital age, where everything is available 24/7, the opportunity to shop your feelings is always just a click away.

Emotional Check-Ins: The Pause Before You Purchase

So, how do you break the emotional spending cycle without depriving yourself entirely? It starts with awareness—and a willingness to pause. The goal isn't to eliminate all indulgence but to make sure your purchases are intentional, not impulsive.

Before you hit "buy," ask yourself these quick questions:

What am I feeling right now? Are you genuinely in need of what you're buying, or are you using it to soothe boredom, stress, or sadness?

Will this matter tomorrow? Impulse buys feel urgent in the moment, but most lose their allure quickly. If you wouldn't care about it in 24 hours, it's probably not worth it.

Is this a treat or a trigger? There's a difference between rewarding yourself and emotionally numbing. Make sure your "treats" are genuine joys, not quick fixes.

Can I afford this comfortably? If a purchase is going to create stress later—whether it's credit card guilt or cutting into your essentials—it's probably not worth the temporary high.

Am I in control, or is my mood calling the shots? If your spending feels reactive, take a breather. Delaying a purchase for even 24 hours can break the emotional spell.

Practicing these check-ins helps you rewire your spending habits. Over time, you'll start to recognize your emotional triggers and make decisions from a place of intention rather than impulse.

At the heart of it, emotional spending is about seeking

comfort. And while there's nothing wrong with treating yourself, true comfort doesn't come from a shopping cart. It comes from knowing you're in control of your money—not the other way around.

When you start recognizing how your feelings influence your spending, you reclaim that control. You can still enjoy indulgences without letting your emotions hijack your financial goals. Because the best kind of spending? It's the kind that feels good long after the dopamine fades.

10

Rich Friends, Broke Feelings

AN INVITE TO A FANCY brunch, a last-minute group vacation, or a friend casually suggesting an upscale dinner like it's no big deal. For them, it probably isn't. But for you? Every "yes" feels like a ticking time bomb for your bank account. If you've ever winced at a Venmo request or silently panicked when the bill hits the table, you already know: being the "broke" friend in a circle where money flows like champagne isn't just financially draining—it's emotionally exhausting.

Here's the truth no one says out loud: money tension in friendships is *real*. And when your friends live on a different financial wavelength, even the best relationships can feel like a minefield. It's not that you don't want to be there for every bougie brunch and destination wedding—sometimes, you simply can't. But saying "I can't afford it" in a world that glorifies excess can feel like admitting failure.

Still, you shouldn't have to choose between protecting your wallet and keeping your friendships. The real flex? Learning how to maintain your financial boundaries without sacrificing the relationships that matter. And if done right, you might even inspire your circle to rethink their spending habits, too.

When Their Budget Isn't Your Budget

It's easy to feel like the odd one out when your friends drop cash like it's pocket change while you're tracking your every expense. But here's a reality check: everyone has a financial limit—it's just not always visible. Maybe your friend who's always jet-setting is drowning in credit card debt. Maybe that "casual" luxury they flaunt is bankrolled by family wealth. You can't always see the full picture, and comparing your behind-the-scenes reality to someone else's highlight reel will only drive you crazy.

Still, knowing this doesn't make it easier when you're invited to events that feel out of reach. And the pressure to keep up isn't just financial—it's emotional. You worry that saying no will make you seem stingy or that setting a spending limit will paint you as the "cheap" friend. But here's the thing: true friendships aren't built on shared tax brackets. If your value to the group hinges on how much you can spend, it's time to rethink the dynamic.

Normalizing Financial Transparency

The awkward truth? Most people aren't comfortable talking about money, even with their closest friends. But the silence around finances is what breeds the most pressure. If you've ever felt isolated while trying to keep up, imagine how many of your friends are quietly feeling the same way. Someone has to break the ice—and it might as well be you.

Start by reframing how you think about these conversations. Setting financial boundaries isn't about making excuses; it's about owning your choices. And when you approach it with confidence, it makes it easier for others to do the same.

You don't need to offer a detailed breakdown of your financial situation. A simple, "Hey, I'm watching my spending right now—

can we find something more low-key?" is enough. The more casual and straightforward you are, the less awkward it becomes. And if your friends are the real deal, they'll respect you for being honest instead of pretending to afford a lifestyle that doesn't align with your reality.

The Art of Saying "No" Without Guilt

There's an art to turning down pricey plans without feeling like a buzzkill. And it starts with understanding that your financial health isn't up for debate. You don't owe anyone an apology for prioritizing your goals—and you definitely shouldn't be losing sleep over declining a $200 dinner.

If the idea of saying "I can't afford it" feels too raw, try reframing the language. Instead of "I can't," say, "I'm choosing not to spend on that right now." This subtle shift turns your decision into a personal boundary rather than a limitation. You're not saying you're incapable—you're saying you're intentional.

And if you want to soften the blow? Offer an alternative. "I'm skipping the trip, but I'd love to plan a cozy weekend hang instead" keeps the connection intact without the financial strain. It also signals that your "no" isn't a rejection of the friendship—it's just a different way of showing up.

When You're the Only One Budgeting

Let's be real—sometimes, being the "budgeting" friend in a lavish circle can feel like you're speaking a different language. You're the one calculating how much those bottomless mimosas will cost after tax and tip while everyone else is waving the server over for another round. And the deeper you go into your financial journey, the clearer the divide can feel.

But here's the plot twist: you don't need your friends to be on the same financial page—you just need them to respect the one you're on. The right people will understand if you're choosing to skip an event or cap your spending. And the wrong people? Well, that's a different conversation.

If you feel like your financial boundaries aren't being respected, it's okay to address it directly. Try something simple, like: "I love hanging out with you guys, but some of these plans are out of my budget. Can we find things to do that work for everyone?" If they brush it off or make you feel uncomfortable, that says more about them than it does about you.

Friendships Built on More Than Money

At the end of the day, the strongest friendships aren't built on shared spending habits—they're built on shared values. The friends who matter will care more about your presence than your contribution to the bill. And the ones who don't? Well, they were never really your people.

Protecting your wallet doesn't make you cheap—it makes you smart. And true friends will value you for who you are, not for how much you're willing to spend. The real flex? Knowing your worth—and realizing that no price tag can define it.

Because here's the truth: you don't need to keep up to belong. Your value isn't measured by your bank balance, and your friendships shouldn't hinge on your ability to afford the next expensive outing. The people who genuinely care about you will understand that. And if they don't? You're better off spending your time—and your money—elsewhere.

PART 3

Everyday Strategies to Save Without Stress

11

The Subscription Purge

SUBSCRIPTIONS ARE LIKE GLITTER—THEY SNEAK in quietly and stick around long after they should be gone. At first, it's harmless. A streaming service to binge your favorite show. A fitness app because, hey, this might finally be the year you become a Pilates girlie. Maybe a monthly beauty box because self-care is essential, right? But here's the thing—those little charges, the ones that feel almost invisible when they hit your bank account, add up fast. And the worst part? You don't even notice them until your statement looks like a catalog of services you barely remember signing up for.

Companies aren't just hoping you'll forget—they're banking on it. Automatic payments are designed to be frictionless, which makes spending money feel effortless. You don't even have to lift a finger. The convenience is addictive because who wants to manually pay bills when you could have everything on autopilot? But there's a dark side to the ease—when payments become invisible, your awareness of them disappears too. What's a few dollars here and there? Not much, until you're paying hundreds annually for things you never use.

Here's a wake-up call: The average person spends $219 per month on subscriptions—and that number is rising. From meal kits to meditation apps, everything comes with a recurring charge.

And those "free trials"? They aren't free if you forget to cancel. Businesses know that once your card is on file, inertia takes over. It's not just laziness—it's a psychological game. The easier it is to start a subscription, the harder they make it to leave.

Why Subscriptions Feel So Painless

Ever wonder why handing over cash feels more painful than tapping your phone? It's all about the psychology of spending. Physical money triggers a sense of loss—when you part with actual bills, your brain feels it. Digital transactions, on the other hand, are abstract. The same brain that cringes when you break a $50 barely flinches when a $12.99 charge quietly pulls from your bank account each month. And businesses love that.

Subscription models weren't always the norm. Back in the day, you bought things once and owned them forever—music, movies, even gym memberships. Now, everything's a recurring cost. It's more profitable for companies to charge you indefinitely than to make a one-time sale. Even essentials like software have moved to the subscription model. That Adobe Photoshop license you'd buy once? Now it's a monthly bill.

And here's the kicker—the more invisible the payment, the less you question it. Automatic renewals keep you locked in because there's no urgency to reassess. When was the last time you actually reviewed every subscription hitting your account? Exactly.

The Silent Leak in Your Bank Account

The scariest thing about subscriptions isn't the big ones—it's the tiny, forgettable ones. That $4.99 charge for a meditation app you downloaded during a mental health spiral. The "free trial" that turned into a $15.99 monthly drain. You don't notice the slow leak, but it's there. And those seemingly harmless amounts? They add up to **thousands per year.**

Think of it like a dripping faucet. A drip doesn't seem like much—but over time, it fills the sink and floods the room. Subscriptions work the same way. A little here, a little there—until your paycheck is vanishing before you've even had your morning coffee.

If you want to stop the financial bleeding, you need to do a **subscription audit**—and you need to be relentless.

The Audit: Taking Back Control

Step one? Face the truth. Open your bank and credit card statements and **go line by line**. Every charge matters—no skipping, no excuses. Make a list of every recurring payment. If you want to be extra thorough (and you should), check platforms like PayPal and Apple Pay—sneaky charges often hide there.

Now, here's where you get brutal. For each subscription, ask yourself:

> *Do I actually use this?* If you can't remember the last time you logged in, it's time to cut it loose.
> *Does this improve my life?* If it's not adding real value, why keep it?
> *Would I miss it if it were gone?* Be honest—if the answer is no, cancel it.

If it's not a clear **yes**, it's a **no**.

Why Canceling Feels So Hard

Here's the thing: Canceling subscriptions is intentionally annoying. Companies make sign-ups a breeze but bury cancellation buttons behind a maze of menus. Some even force you to call during "business hours" (because who has time for that?). And let's not even talk about those guilt-trip pop-ups—"Are you *sure* you want to leave? You'll miss out on so much!"

But you're not falling for that anymore. You know the game. If a company makes canceling hard, they're showing you where their priorities lie—and it's not with you.

Pro tip? Use services like **Rocket Money** or **Subby** to track and cancel subscriptions effortlessly. If you're tired of playing hide-and-seek with "cancel" buttons, these tools do the heavy lifting.

The Emotional Side of Letting Go

Cutting subscriptions isn't just a financial decision—it's an emotional one. There's a weird attachment to services, even if we barely use them. That yoga app? It represents the future version of you who works out every morning. That digital magazine? Proof you're still the kind of person who stays informed—even if it's been months since you opened it.

But here's the truth: Holding onto things you don't use won't make you that person. Keeping a subscription doesn't create a lifestyle—it just creates a recurring charge. If it's not actively improving your life, it's holding you back.

When to Keep Paying (Because Not Everything Needs to Go)

Not all subscriptions are the enemy. Some are worth every penny—if they align with your actual needs and values. The key is **intentional spending**. If it saves you time, genuinely brings joy, or supports your well-being, keep it.

Think about:

- **Services that save time:** Grocery delivery or productivity tools
- **Investments in growth:** Educational platforms or fitness

memberships you *actually use*
- **Intentional entertainment:** That one streaming service you genuinely enjoy

It's not about living a subscription-free life—it's about keeping only what serves you.

To avoid subscription creep in the future, follow a simple rule: **If you can't track it, you can't keep it.** Set a calendar reminder to review subscriptions every three months. Be proactive about checking for hidden renewals, and always assess if what you're paying for still fits your lifestyle.

Also, watch out for "annual commitment" traps. Companies offer discounts if you pay upfront—but if you're not 100% sure you'll use it all year, that "deal" becomes deadweight.

Subscription creep isn't just a money problem—it's a **power problem**. Every time a company quietly charges your card, they're taking a piece of your financial freedom. But by auditing, cutting, and being intentional, you reclaim that power. Your money should work for you—not the other way around.

It's your bank account. It's time to take charge.

12

Impulse-Proof Your Life

IMPULSE SPENDING ISN'T JUST A "bad habit"—it's a whole psychological playground, and trust me, companies know exactly how to keep you playing. That sudden rush to click "buy now" feels harmless in the moment. A scented candle here, a random kitchen gadget there—after all, it's not like you're dropping thousands at once. But those little splurges, the ones you barely think twice about, are often the biggest leaks in your bank account. And the kicker? Most of the time, you don't even *want* the stuff a week later.

If you've ever opened a package and thought, "Why did I even buy this?"—you're not alone. In the age of one-click purchases and same-day delivery, resisting temptation is harder than ever. Brands don't just sell products—they sell urgency, convenience, and the promise of a happier, more fabulous version of you. And impulse purchases? They're the emotional candy companies dangle right at your fingertips.

But here's the truth: You're not powerless against those perfectly timed ads and flash sales. Impulse-proofing your life isn't about deprivation—it's about **buying with intention**. And once you learn how to break the cycle, you'll realize that those fleeting urges don't control you. You control them.

The Brain Science Behind Impulse Spending

Let's start with a little brain chemistry lesson—don't worry, no lab coats required. Every time you make a purchase, your brain lights up with a rush of **dopamine**—a neurotransmitter linked to pleasure and reward. This is the same chemical that fires when you eat chocolate or get a compliment. But here's the twist: The dopamine spike doesn't come from owning the thing—it comes from the *anticipation* of getting it.

This is why online shopping feels so addictive. The thrill isn't about using your new skincare set—it's about the rush you feel hitting "add to cart." And when your brain is in that reward-seeking mode, logic takes a backseat. You're not thinking about your budget or whether you actually need a fifth pair of black boots—you're chasing that chemical high.

And brands? They're not playing fair. Every design choice on a shopping site is carefully crafted to exploit your brain's reward system. The countdown timers. The "only 3 left!" alerts. The bright red SALE banners. These aren't random—they're psychological triggers designed to override your self-control and make you spend fast.

Impulse spending isn't about willpower—it's about chemistry. And the first step to impulse-proofing your life is recognizing that the system is rigged.

Why Delayed Gratification Works (and Isn't Boring)

If dopamine is the gas pedal driving your spending, delayed gratification is the brake. It's the ability to pause, sit with your desire, and decide if the purchase is actually worth it. Sounds simple, right? But in a world where you can buy anything in seconds, waiting feels countercultural.

Here's the magic of delayed gratification: **It lets the emotional high wear off.** That irresistible urge to buy something is usually temporary. By waiting—whether it's 24 hours or a full week—you give your brain time to cool down. And once the initial excitement fades, you'll often realize you didn't want the thing as much as you thought.

Studies show that people who practice delayed gratification not only save more money—they feel more **satisfied** with their purchases. When you stop reacting to every impulse, you become a more intentional consumer. You're no longer chasing momentary highs—you're investing in things that genuinely add value to your life.

And no, delayed gratification doesn't mean never buying fun things. It just means you're **choosing** them consciously rather than reacting on autopilot.

Impulse Triggers

Impulse spending isn't random—it's emotional. Certain feelings, situations, and even environments can trigger that "must-buy" reflex. If you want to curb the habit, you need to identify your triggers. Here are some of the sneakiest culprits:

Emotional Shopping – Feeling stressed, bored, or anxious? Retail therapy promises a quick dopamine hit to numb the discomfort.

Social Media Influence – That influencer making a face mask look life-changing? You're not immune to the power of "if they have it, I should too."

Scarcity Mindset – Limited-time offers and "last chance" sales make you panic-buy things you'd otherwise ignore.

Convenience Culture – One-click ordering removes friction, making purchases feel easy—and easier to forget about later.

Comparison Pressure – Seeing friends' shopping hauls can trigger the fear of missing out, making you spend to "keep up."

Understanding what drives your impulse spending is half the battle. The other half? Learning how to hit **pause** before you spiral.

The 24-Hour Rule: Your Impulse Cure

Enter your new best friend: The 24-hour rule. It's as simple as it sounds—when you feel the urge to impulse buy, wait 24 hours before making a decision. This isn't about punishing yourself—it's about giving your brain time to recalibrate.

Here's why it works:

It interrupts emotional spending. That immediate buzz starts to fade, helping you think more clearly.

It reveals true wants vs. fleeting desires. If you still want it after 24 hours, it's likely a more intentional purchase.

It gives you time to check your budget. No more surprise "how did I spend this much?" moments.

Want to take it up a notch? For larger purchases, try a **7-day rule**. If it's not an essential and it costs over a certain amount (say, $100), sit with the decision for a full week. This extra cushion ensures you're making mindful, not impulsive, choices.

How to Press Pause on Impulse Spending (Without Feeling Deprived)

Impulse-proofing your life isn't about saying "no" to everything—it's about creating systems that give you control. Here's how to start:

Create a "Want List" – Instead of buying immediately, add desired items to a list. Revisit it weekly to see what still feels worth it.

Unsubscribe from Temptation – Those promo emails?

Unsubscribe. Out of sight, out of mind.

Use Cash for Extras – When you pay with physical money, your brain registers the loss. Reserve cards for essentials only.

Budget for Splurges – Give yourself a "fun fund" each month for non-essentials. When it's gone, it's gone.

Ask Future You – Will this purchase still make sense a month from now? If not, it's probably an impulse.

Impulse-proofing isn't about restriction—it's about **freedom**. When you learn to control your spending impulses, you're not just saving money—you're reclaiming agency over your life. No more random Amazon binges. No more post-purchase guilt. Just intentional, empowered choices that actually align with who you are and what you value.

And the best part? When you stop throwing cash at things you barely want, you free up resources for what actually matters—whether that's saving for the future, investing in experiences, or treating yourself to something that feels genuinely worth it.

Because let's be real—your money should work for *you*, not your impulses. And once you master the art of pressing pause, there's no stopping what you can do.

13

Traveling Without the Tourist Debt

TRAVELING FEELS LIKE THE ULTIMATE flex—sunset views, Instagram stories, and the sweet satisfaction of jetting off while everyone else is stuck in the daily grind. But what no one posts is the aftershock when reality hits: credit card statements bloated with "treat yourself" indulgences, mysterious charges you swear you didn't make, and the creeping anxiety that comes with knowing your dreamy escape is dragging your bank account down to reality.

Let's be clear—traveling isn't the problem. It's how we've been conditioned to approach it. The pressure to "go big or stay home" fuels a toxic mix of FOMO and financial recklessness. You're sold the idea that a vacation isn't *worth it* unless it's extravagant. But here's the twist: luxury doesn't have to mean blowing through your savings. You can sip cocktails on a beach, explore new cities, and collect experiences without drowning in tourist debt. The trick? Being smarter about how and when you spend.

Travel is emotional—plain and simple. It's not just about the destination; it's about how that destination makes you *feel*. When you book a trip, you're buying into a fantasy: the version of you who's carefree, adventurous, and effortlessly glamorous. That emotional pull is powerful—and brands know it.

Everything from flashy resort ads to influencer-curated itineraries taps into the fantasy, making you believe that happiness comes with a hefty price tag. Suddenly, "budget travel" feels like settling, and before you know it, you're dropping extra cash on premium seats and $25 airport lattes.

But here's the thing: overspending on a trip doesn't make the memories better—it just makes the aftermath worse. And nothing kills post-vacation bliss faster than the realization that you'll be paying it off for months.

So, how do you escape the tourist debt trap without giving up your travel dreams? It starts by shifting your mindset—from impulsive spending to intentional planning.

The Art of Pre-Trip Budgeting (Without Killing the Vibe)

A travel budget doesn't have to feel like a buzzkill. In fact, knowing your financial boundaries before you leave actually gives you more freedom. When you decide upfront where you're willing to splurge and where you'll save, you're not constantly second-guessing every expense. You're free to enjoy the experience without worrying about the financial hangover later.

Start by breaking your trip into categories:

1. **Non-Negotiables** – What matters most? Maybe it's a fancy hotel, or maybe it's a foodie tour through hidden alleys. Identify the experiences you'll happily spend on.
2. **Flex Items** – These are the "nice-to-haves" that won't make or break the trip. Think room upgrades, last-minute souvenirs, or airport luxuries.
3. **Hard Passes** – What doesn't matter to you? Skip the overpriced tourist traps and focus on experiences that feel worth it.

When you decide these priorities in advance, you're not caught off guard by shiny extras. You're spending intentionally, not emotionally.

Flights, Stays, and Saving Smarter

Let's talk logistics—because no matter how dreamy the destination, the costs add up fast. The secret to saving on flights and stays isn't about finding a random "hot deal"—it's about **timing, strategy, and knowing where to look.**

Book Smart, Not Fast. Last-minute deals? A myth. Flights are cheapest 1-3 months in advance for domestic travel and 3-6 months for international trips. Set flight alerts, and be flexible with dates if you can.

The Accommodation Hack. Ditch the assumption that hotels are always pricier. Sometimes, a boutique hotel with breakfast included is cheaper (and better) than a no-frills Airbnb. Always compare across platforms—and don't sleep on loyalty programs.

Travel Like a Local. Tourist-heavy areas mean higher prices. Stay just outside major hubs for lower rates, better food, and fewer tourist traps.

Points Are Your Best Friend. If you're not using travel rewards or cashback cards, you're leaving money on the table. Rack up points on daily spending and cash them in when wanderlust strikes.

Splurge vs. Save

The "YOLO" mentality hits hardest on vacation—but not every splurge is worth the swipe. Knowing where to spend and where to cut back can stretch your travel budget without sacrificing the fun.

When to Splurge:

- Unique Experiences – That once-in-a-lifetime hot air balloon ride? Worth it.
- Comfort Upgrades (Sometimes) – Long-haul flight? A seat with legroom could save your sanity.
- Local Cuisine – Skip the chain restaurants. Authentic meals are worth every penny.

When to Save:

- Tourist Traps – Overpriced attractions with long lines? Hard pass.
- Souvenirs – Unless it's meaningful, that "I ❤ [City]" mug will collect dust.
- Convenience Fees – Taxis from the airport and minibar snacks? Not worth it.

Post-Trip Financial Recovery (Without the Panic)

You've unpacked, uploaded the photo dumps, and—uh oh—your credit card statement just hit. If you overspent (it happens), don't spiral. A financial reset can soften the blow and get you back on track.

Before the post-trip guilt kicks in, review your purchases. Spotting where the money actually went helps you plan smarter next time. Shift your next month's spending to cover any excess. Cut back on dining out or non-essentials until your balance rebounds. If you used credit, prioritize paying off high-interest purchases first. Even small extra payments each month will save you from drowning in interest. Start replenishing your travel savings right away—so your next adventure doesn't come with financial anxiety.

Traveling isn't just about collecting passport stamps—it's about creating moments that enrich your life. And the best memories? They're not tied to the most expensive choices.

When you approach travel with financial clarity, you're not giving up indulgence—you're **choosing it intentionally.** You get to enjoy the best of both worlds: the thrill of exploration *and* the peace of mind that comes with knowing your bank account is still intact.

Because real luxury? It's not just about where you go—it's about knowing you can afford the life you love, both on vacation and when you're back home. And once you master that balance, the world is yours.

14

When Fun Costs Too Much

THERE'S A QUIET PANIC THAT hits when you check your bank balance after a weekend of "just one more round." What started as a casual Friday night spiraled into brunch plans, an impromptu shopping spree, and Uber receipts that sting. By Sunday evening, you're full of regrets—and not just about the questionable karaoke performance. Somehow, fun always ends up costing more than you planned.

It's no secret: socializing is expensive. Between the rise of $7 lattes and "experiences" that double as Instagram content, the pressure to keep up is relentless. The modern social calendar isn't just about showing up—it's about showing out. And when your friends are booking bottomless brunches, group trips, and spontaneous nights out, the fear of missing out has a direct line to your wallet.

But here's the truth—having fun shouldn't come with a financial hangover. You can live your best life without burning through your savings. The real flex isn't dropping cash without a second thought; it's knowing how to enjoy yourself without the side of spending guilt.

Why We Spend More When We're Having Fun

There's something about a good time that makes us reckless with our money. Psychologists call it the "hot state"—when emotions take over, logical decision-making goes out the window. You're not thinking about your budget when you're caught up in the vibe; you're thinking about how good that next cocktail will taste or how easy it is to Venmo your share and keep the night rolling.

Social spending is also tied to emotional validation. When you say yes to every invite, there's a sense of belonging. Declining plans feels like rejecting connection, and nobody wants to be the person who can't keep up. So, you convince yourself that "it's just this once"—until that excuse becomes a monthly tradition.

Adding to the problem? The unspoken competition of who's living the most glamorous life. In a world where curated highlight reels flood your feed, there's a subconscious pressure to match that energy. You start equating joy with consumption—thinking you need to spend more to prove you're living fully.

But here's the catch: the best memories aren't always the most expensive ones. And while money can buy access, it doesn't guarantee happiness. At some point, you have to ask—are you paying for fun or just paying to keep up?

When "No" Feels Awkward

One of the hardest things about reining in social spending is the guilt. Turning down plans feels like a confession—like admitting you're broke, boring, or both. But here's the thing: setting financial boundaries isn't a personality flaw. You don't owe anyone an explanation for protecting your peace (or your wallet).

The key is learning how to say "no" without making it weird. You don't need to fake a busy schedule or invent excuses. Honesty, when delivered with confidence, sets the tone. If your friends can't respect that, the problem isn't your budget—it's your circle.

If you're feeling stuck, try this:

"I'm down to hang, but I'm keeping it low-key this month. What about a coffee catch-up instead?"
"That sounds amazing, but I'm saving for something big—can we plan something chill?"
"I'd love to join, but I'm watching my spending right now. Let's do something fun that doesn't break the bank!"

When you own your financial choices without apology, you shift the energy. You're not being cheap—you're being intentional. And more often than not, your honesty opens the door for others to admit they're feeling the pressure too.

Finding Joy Without the Price Tag

Here's a wild thought—what if fun didn't always require a credit card swipe? It's easy to get stuck in the mindset that "real" enjoyment comes with a hefty bill, but that's just consumer culture talking. The most fulfilling experiences? They're usually free (or at least budget-friendly).

Start by redefining what fun actually means to you. Is it about connection? Creativity? Exploration? Once you know what feeds your soul, you can find ways to do that without emptying your wallet. Some of the most memorable moments come from simple pleasures—a sunset picnic, a spontaneous dance party in your living room, or deep conversations that stretch late into the night.

You don't have to quit socializing—you just need to get smarter about it. Host potlucks instead of pricey dinners. Swap fancy cocktail bars for rooftop BYOB hangs. Plan themed movie nights, park meet-ups, or game nights where the real currency is laughter, not money. Fun isn't about what you spend—it's about who you're with and how present you are in the moment.

Recovering from Social Spending

If you've already fallen into the "fun costs too much" trap, don't spiral. You can reset without swearing off social life entirely. The trick is acknowledging where things went off track and making intentional tweaks moving forward.

First, audit your last few social outings. Where did the money actually go? Was it spontaneous splurges, pressure to keep up, or convenience spending? Knowing your patterns helps you spot weak points before they become budget blowouts.

Next, set a realistic "fun fund." Instead of feeling guilty about every social expense, allocate a monthly amount that fits your goals. When the fund runs out, you get creative—or hit pause until next month. This way, you can enjoy life while staying in control.

Finally, don't let one expensive weekend define your financial future. If you overspent, adjust without punishing yourself. Cut back on non-essential spending for a few weeks, redirect extra cash toward covering the gap, and remind yourself that one slip-up doesn't erase your progress.

At the end of the day, fun doesn't have to cost you your financial peace. True luxury is knowing you can enjoy life without being shackled to debt or anxiety. It's about finding a balance where you can say yes to joy without sacrificing your future.

When you realize that your worth isn't tied to how much you spend, you start making choices from a place of empowerment—not pressure. And that? That's the kind of freedom money can't buy.

15

The No-Spend Experiment

THERE'S A THRILL IN SWIPING your card—a tiny rush of satisfaction with every click of "add to cart" or the smooth tap of your phone against a payment reader. It feels effortless, a seamless part of modern life, until the numbers start adding up in a way that feels… less thrilling. Before you know it, a week of "harmless" indulgences turns into a month of wondering where your money actually went.

That's where the no-spend experiment comes in. It's not about punishing yourself or living like a minimalist monk. It's about hitting pause on mindless spending, giving yourself the space to see where your money goes—and more importantly, why. It's not as extreme as it sounds. You're not banning all purchases or swearing off every little joy. Instead, you're making a conscious decision to stop the auto-pilot spending and figure out what truly adds value to your life.

At first glance, a no-spend challenge feels like a financial detox—a way to cleanse yourself of all the little leaks draining your bank account. But it's also a mirror. It reflects how much of your spending is habit, how much is emotional, and how much is just… unnecessary. The first week can be a revelation, and if you're honest with yourself, it's not just about the money. It's about realizing how often spending is a reflex—a distraction when you're bored, a reward when you're stressed, or a social crutch when you don't want to be the person who says no.

A no-spend experiment isn't just about cutting costs—it's about clarity. It forces you to face the real motivations behind your purchases. Are you shopping because you actually need something? Or because you're chasing a quick hit of happiness? It's easy to convince yourself that those daily coffee runs and Friday-night takeouts are "deserved." And maybe they are. But when those small, seemingly harmless habits compound, they quietly drain the potential from your paycheck.

Breaking the Auto-Spend Cycle

Modern spending is designed to be frictionless. Companies invest millions in making it easier for you to part with your cash—one-click checkouts, subscription models, "buy now, pay later" schemes. The less you think about it, the more you spend. That's why a no-spend experiment feels so radical—it forces you to slow down and disrupt the cycle.

At first, it's awkward. You notice how often you reach for your phone to order food when cooking feels like a hassle. You catch yourself clicking through sales emails out of habit, even when you don't need anything. It's like realizing how many times a day you check social media without thinking—it's unconscious until you make it conscious.

And that's the magic of the no-spend challenge—it brings every spending decision to the surface. It asks you to confront the difference between real needs and emotional wants. You start to see where your money goes—not just the numbers, but the patterns behind them.

The Emotional Edge of Not Spending

The hardest part of a no-spend experiment isn't the money—it's the feelings that surface when you stop spending. Because for most people, money isn't just about transactions—it's about emotions. Spending is woven into how we soothe ourselves, how we bond with others, how we express joy or mask pain.

When you remove the easy comfort of buying something, what's left? Maybe it's boredom. Maybe it's the restlessness of wanting something new to break up the monotony. Maybe it's the anxiety that bubbles up when you're not distracting yourself with the next little treat.

The emotional weight of not spending is where the real work begins. It's about noticing when you feel the itch to spend—noticing what triggers it and sitting with that feeling instead of numbing it with a purchase. That's why a no-spend experiment is more than a budgeting tool—it's an emotional detox. It reveals how much of your spending is about managing feelings rather than meeting actual needs.

Making It Sustainable (Without Losing Your Mind)

Let's be clear—this isn't about living a joyless, monk-like existence. You don't need to give up everything you love or cut yourself off from life's pleasures. The goal isn't deprivation—it's mindfulness. It's about understanding where your money goes and deciding what genuinely deserves it. One of the best ways to keep a no-spend challenge from feeling miserable is to shift the focus. Instead of thinking about what you can't do, focus on what you can. What experiences are free but still bring you joy? What hobbies can you revisit that don't cost a penny? Who in your life makes you feel good without needing a fancy setting?

When spending isn't an option, creativity steps in. Maybe that means trading takeout for a homemade dinner with friends. Swapping a pricey night out for a cozy movie marathon. Rediscovering simple joys—like a sunset walk, a good book, or an afternoon of music and journaling.

The best part? You start realizing that many of the things you thought required spending actually don't. The world doesn't stop spinning just because you skip happy hour or decline another retail therapy session. And the confidence you gain from knowing you can enjoy life without constantly spending? That's priceless.

What Happens When You Finish?

Here's the real kicker: the end of a no-spend challenge isn't just about saving money—it's about knowing yourself better. You walk away with a sharper awareness of your spending triggers and a clearer sense of what really brings you happiness.

You might realize that half of what you used to buy was just noise—stuff that filled the moment but didn't improve your life. Or you might discover that there are a few things truly worth the splurge—things that add real value and joy. And when you spend again, you do it from a place of intention rather than impulse. A successful no-spend experiment isn't measured by how much you save—it's measured by how much you learn. And the biggest lesson? You're not powerless. You're not trapped in a cycle of endless consumption. You have the ability to make choices that align with your values and your financial future.

When you know you can press pause on spending without your world falling apart, you take back control. And in a culture that constantly pushes you to spend more, that's a radical act of freedom.

16

Shopping Smarter, Not Harder

SHOPPING ISN'T JUST A TRANSACTION—IT'S an experience carefully designed to pull you in, seduce your senses, and gently nudge you into spending more than you ever intended. Every time you step into a store or scroll through an online sale, you're stepping into a carefully crafted psychological playground. And whether it's the warm lighting in a boutique, the limited-time countdown on a website, or that perfectly placed "buy one, get one" display, the game is always the same—get you to part with your cash as easily (and frequently) as possible.

The reality is, most of us aren't making purely rational decisions when we shop. We're emotional beings in a world where marketers have mastered the art of pushing our buttons. It's why you'll convince yourself that a 30% discount on something you didn't even need is a "smart buy" or why that little red clearance sticker can override your better judgment. But here's the twist—once you understand the tricks being played on you, you can flip the script. Shopping smarter isn't about cutting yourself off from nice things; it's about making every purchase feel intentional, worthwhile, and fully in your control.

The Psychology of "Why You Buy"

Stores aren't just selling products—they're selling a feeling. And they know exactly how to craft an environment that taps into your emotions. Ever noticed how grocery stores put the essentials—milk, eggs, bread—at the farthest corner of the store? It's not by accident. You're meant to wander past aisles of impulse buys before you reach the items you actually came for. That leisurely stroll through rows of snacks and novelty treats? It's a trap.

Online shopping plays a similar game but in subtler ways. Flash sales with ticking countdowns create a sense of urgency, making you feel like you'll miss out if you don't act fast. Free shipping thresholds encourage you to toss in a few extra items just to avoid paying for delivery. And those personalized product recommendations? They're not random. Algorithms track your browsing habits and use your own preferences to keep you spending.

The first step in shopping smarter is recognizing these tactics for what they are—psychological nudges designed to override your rational brain. Once you see through the manipulation, you reclaim the power to decide whether a purchase genuinely serves you or just feeds the marketing machine.

The Illusion of a "Good Deal"

Few things are more tempting than a markdown. Seeing a price slashed from £200 to £75 triggers a deep sense of satisfaction—you're not just buying an item, you're winning. But here's the truth: that "deal" might not be as good as it looks.

Retailers know that people love a bargain, and they exploit that by manipulating original prices. Ever wondered why some stores seem to be in a constant state of sale? Often, those discounts are based on inflated "regular" prices that no one was ever expected to pay. By artificially raising the original cost, they make the sale price seem like an irresistible steal. And don't even get started on those "limited-time offers" that mysteriously reappear every month—it's a tactic designed to rush you into buying before you have time to think.

Shopping smarter means asking yourself a simple but powerful question: *Would I want this if it wasn't on sale?* If the answer is no, walk away. A bargain isn't a bargain if you didn't need the item in the first place.

The Art of Intentional Buying

Impulse shopping is easy. Thoughtful, intentional buying takes a bit more effort—but the payoff is worth it. One of the most effective tools for shopping smarter is the creation of a "must-buy" list. This isn't your standard grocery list; it's a running catalogue of things you genuinely need or have been wanting for a while. When you stick to your list, you're far less likely to fall for the siren call of a flashy sale or an impulse purchase.

Think of your must-buy list as a financial filter. It's a way to pause before a purchase and ask yourself: *Is this something I've thought about and genuinely value? Or is it just a passing whim triggered by clever marketing?* This shift in mindset transforms your shopping habits from reactive to intentional—you become the one in charge, not the algorithm or the sales display.

Another power move? Implement a waiting period for non-essential purchases. If you spot something you think you want, give yourself 24 to 48 hours to think it over. More often than not, that initial spark of desire fades once you step away. And if you're still thinking about it a day or two later? That's a sign it might actually be worth your money.

When to Splurge vs. When to Save

Not all spending is bad. In fact, some purchases genuinely enhance your life and are worth every penny. But knowing when to invest and when to save is an art—and one that protects both your finances and your happiness.

Splurge when the purchase adds long-term value to your life. A quality winter coat that will last for years? Worth it. A cheap fast-fashion trend that'll fall apart after two washes? Probably not. Pay for things that align with your values and your lifestyle—experiences that create lasting memories, tools that enhance your work, and pieces that bring everyday comfort and utility.

On the flip side, save on things that are fleeting or easily replaceable. Trendy items that will be "out" by next season, beauty products you'll barely use, or tech gadgets that lose their novelty after a few months—these are the areas where cutting costs makes the most sense. When in doubt, ask yourself: *Is this purchase supporting the life I want to live, or just filling a temporary void?*

The Power of Conscious Consumption

Shopping smarter isn't about deprivation—it's about shifting your relationship with spending from impulsive to intentional. It's about knowing the difference between a want and a need, understanding the psychology behind why you buy, and giving yourself permission to make purchases that genuinely enhance your life.

When you become a conscious consumer, you're no longer a passive player in the game of retail manipulation. You're in control. You decide what's worth your money, your time, and your attention. And that kind of power? It feels a whole lot better than a quick dopamine hit from a flash sale.

Because at the end of the day, smart shopping isn't about having more—it's about having what truly matters. And once you start making your purchases with purpose, you'll realize that you were never really missing out by spending less—you were gaining freedom.

PART 4

Saving Big for Big Dreams

17

The Future You Fund

PICTURE THIS: IT'S A FEW years down the line, and you're unlocking the front door of a place you can finally call your own. Or maybe you're tossing your suitcase into the trunk of a sleek new car—one that doesn't rattle when you hit 40 mph. These big milestones—homes, cars, dream vacations, even early retirement—aren't just wishful thinking. They're entirely possible, but only if you start building a financial future that your "someday self" will thank you for. And no, this isn't about skipping every latte or surviving on instant noodles. It's about making smart, sustainable moves now that will quietly stack up into something huge later.

The truth? Most people want the big, shiny life moments, but they get stuck in the trap of "I'll save later." Later, when you earn more. Later, when things are less hectic. Later, when that magical version of you appears—fully organized, financially disciplined, and effortlessly wealthy. But here's the hard pill: *later* rarely shows up the way you imagine. Life has a funny way of handing you new expenses, new responsibilities, and a never-ending list of reasons to put saving on the back burner. If you wait for the "perfect" time to save, you'll be waiting forever.

Why "Later" is a Liar

Delaying saving is like hitting snooze on your dreams. Sure, it feels harmless in the moment—comforting, even. But while you're waiting for the perfect time to start, you're missing out on the most powerful financial advantage there is: *time itself.*

Here's the thing: saving isn't just about the amount you put away—it's about how long that money has to grow. Enter compound interest, the magical force that can turn small, consistent savings into life-changing sums. Every pound you save today has the potential to earn interest, and that interest earns even more interest over time. It's like planting a tree—the sooner you plant, the bigger the shade later.

Let's break it down: If you save £100 a month starting at age 25, you could have around £150,000 by the time you hit 65 (assuming a modest 6% annual return). Wait until 35 to start saving the same amount? You'd only end up with about £76,000. Time isn't just money—it's double the money.

But beyond the numbers, there's another reality to face: life doesn't get cheaper as you age. If you think you're stretched thin now, imagine juggling childcare, a mortgage, and rising living costs down the line. The future version of you will be grateful—deeply grateful—that you started saving while things were still (somewhat) simple.

Paying Your Future Self First

Saving for big goals doesn't have to mean putting your life on pause. You don't need to give up weekend brunches or unfollow every tempting travel influencer. What you need is a system—one that works in the background while you live your life. And the simplest, most effective system? *Automation.*

Automating your savings takes the decision-making (and

temptation) out of the equation. The idea is simple: set up an automatic transfer to a savings account every time you get paid. When your savings happen without you thinking about it, you're far less likely to "accidentally" spend that money on impulse buys or spontaneous splurges.

The key is to treat your savings like a non-negotiable bill—because, honestly, your future deserves that kind of priority. Start small if you need to. Even £50 or £100 a month adds up over time. And as your income grows, so should your savings. The point isn't to hoard every penny—it's to make saving feel as natural as paying your phone bill or ordering your favourite takeout.

Dream Big, Save Smart

Here's where it gets fun: your "Future You Fund" isn't just about stashing money mindlessly. It's about creating a savings plan that's tied to the life you want. You're not saving for the sake of saving—you're investing in milestones that will make your future feel as good as your present.

Start by getting specific. What are your big goals? A down payment on a flat? A month-long European adventure? Freedom from ever worrying about an emergency car repair again? Vague goals lead to vague savings, so map out exactly what you're working toward and how much you'll need.

Once you have a clear vision, break it into manageable chunks. If your dream vacation costs £5,000, saving that in a lump sum might feel impossible. But £420 a month for a year? Suddenly, it's not so overwhelming.

Pro tip: Separate your goals into individual savings accounts or "buckets." Most banks (and even some budgeting apps) let you create separate digital envelopes for different purposes. When your goals have their own dedicated accounts, it's easier to track progress and stay motivated. There's something ridiculously satisfying about watching your "Dream Apartment" fund grow while your day-to-day spending stays on track.

Balancing Today with Tomorrow

Let's be clear: you don't need to live like a monk to secure your future. A smart savings plan balances *enjoying life now* with *preparing for what's next*. It's about knowing when to say yes, when to pause, and when to invest in things that truly matter.

One way to strike this balance? Create a "guilt-free spending" category. Designate a portion of your budget specifically for indulgences—the nights out, the random shopping sprees, the spontaneous getaways. Knowing you've already earmarked money for fun allows you to enjoy these moments without sabotaging your future goals.

And when you do splurge, let it be intentional. Choose experiences and items that genuinely bring you joy, rather than spending mindlessly to fill a void. There's a massive difference between treating yourself to something meaningful and mindlessly blowing cash because "why not?"

The best part about building a Future You Fund? It creates freedom. It's the ability to say "yes" to opportunities, to walk away from situations that no longer serve you, and to build a life that feels both fulfilling and financially secure.

The sooner you start, the easier the journey becomes. And while the world will always find new ways to tempt you into spending, you'll know that every pound you save isn't a sacrifice—it's a gift to the future version of yourself who's living the dream.

Because here's the real flex: being able to afford the life you want without anxiety lurking in the background. And trust—Future You is going to love that.

18

Debt Detox Without the Drama

DEBT HAS A SNEAKY WAY of becoming part of the background noise in your life. It lingers quietly—until it doesn't. One day, you're casually tapping your card for a coffee, and the next, you're side-eyeing your credit card statement wondering how a few small indulgences turned into a balance that seems impossible to shake. The thing about debt is that it's not just numbers on a screen—it's emotional. It weighs on your decisions, clouds your sense of freedom, and can make the idea of financial independence feel like a distant fantasy.

But here's the truth no one likes to say out loud: you can pay off debt *without* putting your entire life on hold. Forget the idea that being financially responsible means living off rice and beans or saying no to every social invite. You don't need to punish yourself into financial freedom—you just need a strategy that works with your lifestyle, not against it. Debt doesn't have to be a lifelong roommate. You can evict it—without the drama.

Debt isn't just a math problem—it's a mental and emotional one. There's a unique kind of stress that comes from owing money. It's that restless feeling when you know your balance is creeping up while you're trying to live your best life. And let's be honest—sometimes it feels easier to ignore the problem entirely. But the weight doesn't disappear just because you refuse to look at it.

What makes debt tricky is that it often feels tied to your identity. A hefty credit card balance can whisper things like *you're irresponsible* or *you'll never figure this out*. But debt is a circumstance, not a character flaw. Everyone has their reasons—whether it's an unexpected emergency, living costs that spiral out of reach, or the temptation to indulge in a little retail therapy when life gets overwhelming. What matters is what you do next.

It's easy to fall into an all-or-nothing mindset—either you live like a hermit to pay it off faster, or you throw your hands up and keep swiping. Neither extreme is sustainable. The sweet spot is finding a repayment plan that fits your reality—one where you're making real progress without sacrificing every little thing that brings you joy.

Making Debt Payoff Work for You

If the thought of tackling your debt feels overwhelming, you're not alone. The good news? You don't need to become a finance guru overnight. What you *do* need is a clear, realistic plan—one that fits your life without making you miserable.

Start by facing the numbers. Yes, it's intimidating, but clarity is power. Make a list of everything you owe—credit cards, student loans, personal loans, all of it. Knowing your total debt balance, minimum payments, and interest rates gives you a solid foundation to build from. Once you have the full picture, it's time to choose your strategy.

There are two tried-and-true methods for tackling debt: the **snowball method** and the **avalanche method**.

1. **The Snowball Method**: Pay off your smallest debt first while making minimum payments on the rest. This gives you a quick win and a psychological boost to keep going.
2. **The Avalanche Method**: Focus on the debt with the

highest interest rate first, saving you the most money over time.

One isn't better than the other—it's about what works for *you*. If you need the motivation of quick wins, go snowball. If you want to save the most cash in the long run, avalanche is your friend.

The real flex is staying consistent. Automatic payments are your best ally here. Set up auto-transfers for your debt payments so you're chipping away at that balance before you even think about spending on extras. And whenever you come into unexpected money—bonuses, tax refunds, random cash windfalls—consider throwing a chunk toward your debt.

Paying Off Debt Without Pausing Your Life

Here's where most people trip up: they treat paying off debt like a punishment. They cut out every joy, decline every social invite, and end up feeling deprived—and eventually, they burn out. The key to debt detoxing *without* the meltdown is allowing yourself to live while you pay things down.

It's all about balance. Build a "joy budget"—an intentional amount of money set aside for fun while you're tackling debt. It doesn't have to be huge, but knowing you can still grab dinner with friends or treat yourself to something special keeps you from feeling trapped. You're more likely to stick to your repayment plan when you aren't constantly fighting the urge to rebel against it.

And don't let social pressure steer you off course. It's okay to say no to things that don't fit your financial priorities. If your friends are the "let's split the bill evenly" type, suggest alternative plans that won't wreck your budget. Real ones will understand—and if they don't, it's a them problem, not a you problem.

Also, don't sleep on lifestyle tweaks that add up. Cancel subscriptions you barely use, swap out pricey habits for low-cost alternatives, and give yourself permission to pause unnecessary spending. Every little shift counts—and the best part? You're still enjoying life while your debt balance quietly shrinks in the background.

Staying Debt-Free (For Good)

The finish line isn't just about paying off what you owe—it's about staying debt-free long-term. It's easy to slip back into old habits once the pressure's off, but with a few intentional moves, you can keep your financial freedom intact.

First, build yourself a **rainy-day fund**. Nothing throws you back into debt faster than unexpected expenses. Aim to save at least three to six months' worth of essential expenses in an emergency fund. Even a small cushion makes a massive difference when life inevitably throws a curveball.

Second, set healthy spending boundaries. Understand the difference between *want* and *need*, and give yourself time to decide before making major purchases. The rush of a new splurge fades quickly—what sticks around is the balance you have to pay later.

And lastly, celebrate your wins. Every payment is a step toward freedom. Reward yourself when you hit major milestones— whether that's with a small treat, a guilt-free splurge, or just taking a moment to feel proud of how far you've come. You did that. You *earned* that.

Imagine the weight lifting off your shoulders as those balances shrink. Imagine the freedom to make decisions—big and small— without worrying about how much you owe. That future is within reach, and the best part? You don't have to put your life on pause to get there.

Start where you are. Make a plan that fits your world. And as you chip away at your debt—without sacrificing the joy of living— you'll realize that financial freedom isn't just possible. It's inevitable.

19

Emergency Fund, but Make It Fashion

AN EMERGENCY FUND IS LIKE the financial equivalent of a little black dress—timeless, essential, and a total lifesaver when things get messy. Life has a wild sense of humor, and nothing screams "plot twist" like your car breaking down the same month your phone decides to die. Without a backup fund, these moments can easily spiral into credit card chaos, leaving you stressed, scrambling, and wondering why no one warned you that adulthood is basically a series of expensive surprises.

But let's be real—building an emergency fund doesn't exactly scream glamour. It's not as fun as a spontaneous shopping spree or as instantly gratifying as booking a last-minute weekend getaway. Yet, there's something undeniably chic about knowing you're covered if things go sideways. It's not just about saving money—it's about reclaiming control, protecting your peace, and giving yourself the freedom to handle whatever life throws your way without falling into financial panic.

The thing about emergencies? They don't RSVP. They show up uninvited—usually at the worst time—and expect you to foot the bill. And while there's nothing thrilling about stashing cash for a "just-in-case" moment, the alternative is much worse.

Without a cushion, even minor hiccups can become major setbacks.

An emergency fund isn't just for dramatic disasters. Sure, it's there for big-ticket crises like medical bills or sudden job loss—but it also saves you from the annoying (and expensive) realities of everyday life. That chipped tooth after a careless bite of caramel? Covered. The impulse decision to switch jobs and take a month-long breather? Handled. It's not about living in fear of the unexpected—it's about having options when things don't go as planned.

And here's the truth no one tells you: an emergency fund isn't just about protecting your bank account. It protects your mental health. Knowing you have a financial buffer takes the edge off life's uncertainty. It means you can sleep better, breathe easier, and move through life without the constant anxiety that one unexpected bill could send everything crashing down.

Starting Small, Thinking Big

If the thought of saving thousands feels overwhelming, here's your permission to chill. You don't need to build a massive fund overnight. In fact, starting small is the smartest move because it's sustainable. The goal is to build a safety net that grows steadily—one that's realistic for your lifestyle without making you feel deprived.

Begin with a mini-emergency fund—something manageable yet impactful. Even £500 can act as a powerful buffer against life's smaller curveballs. It's enough to cover an urgent repair, a surprise medical co-pay, or an "oops" moment without dipping into your credit card.

Once you hit that milestone, keep the momentum going. Aim for one month's worth of essential expenses next—think rent, utilities, groceries, and basic living costs. From there, work toward the golden rule: three to six months' worth of expenses tucked away in an easily accessible account. It's not about hoarding money—it's about buying yourself breathing room.

Saving Without the Stress

Let's be honest: saving money sounds great in theory, but it can feel like a chore in practice—especially when there are so many tempting ways to spend. The trick is to make building your emergency fund feel effortless, like a casual habit rather than a constant sacrifice.

Automation is your best friend here. Set up an automatic transfer to a separate savings account—preferably one you don't touch for day-to-day expenses. Treat it like a non-negotiable bill that gets paid every month. When saving becomes part of your routine, you're less likely to skip it, and those small, consistent deposits add up faster than you'd think.

And if the idea of sacrificing your social life for savings makes you cringe, here's the good news: you don't have to. Find small, painless ways to redirect money toward your fund. Round-up apps that automatically save spare change from your purchases? Genius. Cash-back rewards that funnel directly into your emergency stash? Even better. It's less about cutting everything fun and more about being intentional with where your money goes.

What Actually Counts as an Emergency?

Here's the thing: not everything that feels urgent is an emergency. That spontaneous designer bag drop? Not an emergency. Your best friend's destination wedding? As much as you love her—it's not a crisis. True emergencies are the unexpected expenses you *can't* avoid—things that directly affect your well-being or ability to function.

Think medical emergencies, essential home or car repairs, sudden job loss, or a last-minute flight for a family crisis. These are the kinds of situations where dipping into your emergency fund makes sense. Anything else? That's what your regular budget is for.

A good rule of thumb: if you can plan for it, it's not an emergency. Annual car maintenance, seasonal wardrobe refreshes, and even birthday gifts—these are predictable costs that deserve their own category in your financial plan. Treat your emergency fund like a sacred, hands-off zone that only gets tapped when life throws an unavoidable curveball.

Flexibility Without Fear

Building an emergency fund isn't about living in fear of the worst—it's about giving yourself the confidence to handle life's unpredictability. It's the quiet kind of luxury—knowing that if things fall apart, you won't.

And the best part? This isn't about choosing between fun and financial security. You can still enjoy the present while preparing for the future. The goal isn't to hoard every penny or live a joyless, budget-obsessed life. It's to create a safety net that supports your ambitions while protecting your peace.

So, think of your emergency fund as the ultimate power move—a quiet flex that says, "I'm ready for whatever comes next." You're not just saving for a rainy day—you're saving for a life where surprises don't shake you. And honestly, that's pretty damn fashionable.

20

Investing: No Suit Required

INVESTING HAS LONG BEEN WRAPPED in an aura of exclusivity—an old boys' club where the language is confusing, the stakes seem high, and the people doing it all seem to have custom suits and a taste for expensive scotch. For decades, the narrative was clear: investing wasn't for everyone. But here's the truth—it's no longer reserved for Wall Street types or spreadsheet enthusiasts. You don't need a finance degree, insider knowledge, or a suit to get started. What you do need is a mindset shift: investing isn't about playing the market; it's about playing for your future.

In a world where a single social media scroll can convince you to spend £100 on a face serum, the idea of stashing money away for some distant "later" can feel...boring. But investing isn't just about retirement—it's about giving your money a job while you live your life. It's how you turn a paycheck into possibilities, whether that means financial freedom, early retirement, or simply not panicking when you think about the future. And the best part? You can start small. You don't need millions to make moves. In fact, the sooner you start—even with pocket change—the better.

Why Your Savings Account Isn't Enough

Keeping all your money in a savings account feels safe, but here's the catch: it's not doing much for you. With inflation quietly gnawing away at the value of your cash, every pound sitting idle is actually losing purchasing power over time. That £50 brunch bill you complain about? In a few years, it could be £75—and your savings won't stretch as far.

Investing flips that narrative. It's about making your money work harder than you do, so it grows while you sleep. The magic behind it all is compound growth—the idea that your returns earn returns. It's a slow burn at first, but over time, it snowballs. What seems like a tiny amount today can grow into something major if you give it time and patience.

The reality is, if you want to live comfortably in the future without sacrificing your current lifestyle, investing isn't optional—it's essential. And no, you don't need to become obsessed with stock charts or spend hours analyzing the market. You just need to start.

The No-BS Guide to Starting Small

The biggest myth about investing is that you need to be rich to do it. Truth is, you can start with the cost of your daily oat latte. Many modern investment platforms—thank you, technology—let you invest with as little as £1. It's not about how much you invest upfront; it's about starting and staying consistent.

Micro-investing apps are an easy on-ramp if you're feeling overwhelmed. They round up your everyday purchases and automatically invest the spare change. Bought an iced coffee for £3.75? They'll round it to £4 and invest the extra 25p. It's barely noticeable, but those small amounts add up over time.

Then there are index funds—the low-maintenance, no-drama way to invest without picking individual stocks. Imagine a basket filled with the biggest companies across industries. When you invest in an index fund, you're buying a tiny slice of all those companies. It's a simple, low-cost way to ride the wave of overall market growth without sweating the daily ups and downs.

Demystifying Investment Jargon

Let's cut through the confusing terminology. You don't need to sound like a finance bro to understand the basics:

- **Stocks**: A piece of ownership in a company. If you own a share of Apple, you literally own a sliver of the company.
- **Bonds**: Essentially, you're lending money to a company or government, and they pay you back with interest. Lower risk, but also lower returns.
- **Index Funds**: These track the overall market (like the S&P 500), offering automatic diversification. Less risk, less hassle.
- **Dividends**: Cash payouts some companies give to shareholders. Think of it as a "thank you" for investing.

You don't need to memorize every term—just know enough to make decisions that align with your financial goals. And spoiler alert: most of those goals don't require day-trading or chasing hot stock tips. They require showing up consistently and thinking long-term.

Playing the Long Game Without Losing Sleep

Investing isn't a get-rich-quick scheme—it's a long game. And if you're waiting for the perfect time to start, you'll wait forever. Market ups and downs are normal, but history shows that those who stay invested for the long haul come out ahead.

The key to stress-free investing? Automate it. Set up a direct debit to an investment account and forget about it. Treat it like a subscription to your future self. Whether it's £20 a month or £200, the consistency matters more than the amount. This strategy, known as dollar-cost averaging, helps you avoid the pressure of trying to "time" the market.

And yes, there will be dips. The market isn't a straight line—it's a rollercoaster. But instead of panicking when things drop, view those moments as an opportunity. If your favourite clothing store had a 20% off sale, you'd stock up—right? The same principle applies to investments. A downturn means you're getting more for your money.

Forget the finance stereotypes. You don't need to trade your personality for a portfolio. Investing isn't about becoming a money-obsessed robot—it's about creating a life where money supports your dreams instead of controlling them.

Maybe your vision of "wealth" isn't a yacht or designer everything—maybe it's the freedom to quit a soul-sucking job, travel on your terms, or support causes you care about. Whatever your goals, investing helps you get there faster and with less stress.

And while the future can feel impossibly far away, the choices you make today shape it. Every pound you invest is a vote for the life you want—one where money isn't a constant worry but a quiet, powerful ally.

So, ditch the suit. Keep your personality. And start investing in a future where you call the shots—no finance degree required.

PART 5

Long-Term Financial Glow-Up

21

The Side Hustle Safety Net

ONCE UPON A TIME, A single paycheck was enough to cover life's essentials, with a little left over for brunch and the occasional splurge. Fast-forward to now, and things look a bit different. Inflation is playing its cruel game, rent keeps rising like it's in a competition, and somehow, streaming subscriptions seem to multiply when you're not looking. Enter the side hustle—a modern-day financial safety net and one of the most practical ways to keep your bank balance from running on fumes. But here's the catch: while side gigs can be a financial lifesaver, they can also be a fast track to burnout if you're not strategic about it.

The beauty of a side hustle isn't just the extra cash—it's the cushion it creates. It's that buffer between you and financial panic when your car decides to break down or your best friend plans a destination wedding. It's also a chance to fund the fun stuff without dipping into your savings. But let's be clear—this isn't about glorifying hustle culture or working yourself to the brink. It's about working smarter, not harder, and making your side gig serve your lifestyle, not the other way around.

Find the hustle that works for you.

Not all side hustles are created equal, and the best one for you depends on two key things: your time and your energy. If you're already stretched thin, the last thing you need is another job that drains you. The goal isn't to trade all your free time for a few extra pounds—it's to find a gig that fits your schedule and plays to your strengths.

For the creatively inclined, selling digital products—think templates, e-books, or even curated playlists—can be a hands-off way to earn once the work is done. If you're more of a social butterfly, offering services like event planning or social media management can turn your natural skills into a steady income stream. And if your idea of a dream job is working from your couch in pyjamas, remote gigs like freelance writing, virtual assistance, or tutoring can keep your earnings up while your commute stays non-existent.

The key is aligning your hustle with your lifestyle. Love to drive? Delivery apps or rideshare services can be an easy win. Always scrolling on social media anyway? Get paid to manage someone else's Instagram feed. Your hustle should enhance your life, not hijack it.

When Hustle Culture Hits Too Hard

There's a fine line between securing the bag and sacrificing your sanity. Social media might glamorize the 24/7 grind, but burnout isn't a badge of humor. The constant push to monetize every hobby or spare minute isn't sustainable—or even necessary. Financial security matters, but so does your mental health.

A smart side hustle fits into your life without consuming it. If your evenings are sacred Netflix time or your weekends are reserved for friends, protect that. Setting boundaries isn't just about your time—it's also about your mental bandwidth. Overcommitting to a side hustle can backfire when the stress outweighs the income.

Be honest about how much time and energy you're willing to

give. Side hustling should feel empowering, not exhausting. If you find yourself dreading your side gig or sacrificing sleep to hit a deadline, it's time to recalibrate. Remember, the goal is to create financial breathing room—not to run yourself into the ground.

The Holy Grail

The ultimate side hustle dream? Making money while you sleep. Passive income sounds like a fantasy, but it's more achievable than you think—if you're willing to play the long game. It's about doing the work upfront and reaping the rewards over time.

Creating digital products is one of the most popular ways to build passive income. Whether it's an online course, stock photos, or downloadable planners, once it's made, it can keep earning indefinitely. Affiliate marketing is another sneaky-good option—if you're already sharing product recommendations with friends, why not earn a commission when they buy?

If you have a little more capital, investing in dividend stocks or rental property can generate ongoing income with minimal maintenance. Even something as simple as high-yield savings accounts or peer-to-peer lending can create passive cash flow without demanding much of your time.

Passive income isn't an overnight fix—it's a slow build. But once those revenue streams are flowing, they offer financial security with less daily hustle. And nothing feels better than waking up to money in your account without lifting a finger.

Making Extra Money Work for You

A side hustle can change your financial reality—but only if you're intentional about how you use that extra cash. It's tempting to treat side hustle income as "fun money," blowing every pound on impulse buys and spontaneous trips. And while there's nothing wrong with a little indulgence, a smarter strategy involves splitting your earnings between immediate gratification and long-term goals.

Think of your side hustle income as an opportunity to speed up your financial timeline. Use it to knock out debt faster, pad your emergency fund, or invest in future-you moves like a retirement account. Even small amounts can have a big impact when you funnel them into the right places.

And here's a pro tip: Automate your side hustle earnings. Set up direct transfers to a separate savings or investment account before you even touch the cash. This "out of sight, out of mind" approach keeps you from spending it all while still allowing room for guilt-free treats.

At the end of the day, your side hustle should be a tool—not a trap. It's there to give you freedom, not take it away. Whether you're using it to cover unexpected expenses, fund your dream vacation, or simply sleep better at night knowing you have a financial cushion, your side hustle works for you—not the other way around.

The beauty of this new economy is that the rules are flexible. You don't need to conform to a rigid, soul-sucking definition of "work" to boost your bank account. You get to decide how much time you give, how much energy you spend, and how much you let your side gig shape your life.

So, hustle if you want to—but on your terms. Let your side gig work as a safety net, a stepping stone, or even a creative outlet. And when the money starts rolling in, remember: You're in control.

22

Credit Score, but Make it Cute

CREDIT SCORES—JUST THE PHRASE ALONE can make your eyes glaze over. It sounds like one of those things grown-ups worry about while sipping black coffee and filing taxes. But here's the truth: your credit score is basically your financial reputation, and in today's world, it holds more power than you think. Want that dreamy apartment? Better have a good score. Eyeing a sleek new car? Your credit score decides if you get the keys or a polite rejection. And the wild part? You don't need a finance degree to master it. With a few smart moves, you can make your credit score work for you—and trust, having a glowing score is the ultimate flex.

Credit scores are not as boring as they sound. Think of your credit score as your financial selfie. It's the snapshot lenders, landlords, and even some employers peek at to judge how responsible you are with money. But unlike a selfie, you can't throw on a filter and fake it—your score is built from your spending and repayment habits, plain and simple.

In most cases, scores range from 300 to 850, and the higher, the better. Anything above 700 is considered good, while a score creeping toward 800? That's next-level responsible. But if your score is sitting closer to 500, don't panic—you're not doomed. Credit is fixable, and you don't have to live in financial purgatory forever.

What really drives your credit score is a mix of factors, but the heavy hitters are your payment history (did you pay your bills on time?), credit utilization (how much credit you're using versus what you're allowed), and your credit age (how long you've had your accounts open). Miss a payment? Your score takes a hit. Max out your credit card? Yep, another dip. But here's the kicker—if you play it smart, you can build (or rebuild) your score faster than you think.

Small Moves, Big Score Energy

Boosting your credit score isn't about drastic changes—it's about consistent, strategic moves that add up over time. And no, you don't need to live like a monk to get results.

Start with the simplest (yet most effective) trick in the book: pay your bills on time. Every. Single. Time. Set reminders, autopay, or even alarms if you must—just don't let a due date slip by. Payment history is the biggest slice of the credit score pie, so treating your due dates like sacred appointments is non-negotiable.

Another sneaky-but-smart hack? Lower your credit utilization. If your credit card limit is £5,000, aim to keep your balance below 30%—that's £1,500 max. And if you really want to impress the credit gods, keep it under 10%. If your balance is creeping up, consider making multiple payments throughout the month to keep your usage low.

And here's an underrated trick: request a credit limit increase. If your spending stays the same while your credit limit rises, your utilization rate drops, and your score climbs. It's a low-effort move with high-reward potential, and many credit card companies let you request an increase online in minutes.

Credit Pitfalls to Dodge

Credit may seem like a game—but it's one where the house always has the edge if you're not careful. Mistakes can stick around like a bad ex, dragging your score down long after the damage is done.

One common trap? Applying for too many credit cards at once. Each time you apply, a "hard inquiry" pings your credit report, and too many in a short period can spook lenders. It's like texting three people at once—someone's going to get suspicious. If you're building credit, stick to one or two cards and keep your spending chill.

Then there's the myth that you should avoid using credit altogether. Big mistake. No credit history is almost as bad as bad credit. Lenders want proof you can handle borrowed money responsibly. Even if you don't *need* to use credit, making small purchases and paying them off immediately shows you're trustworthy.

Also—don't close old credit cards unless absolutely necessary. Credit age plays a major role in your score, and that decade-old card you barely use? It's doing you a favor by keeping your average credit age high. If you really want to minimize risk, keep it open and set a small recurring bill on it to keep it active.

Why Good Credit is the Ultimate Flex

Here's the thing—having a good credit score isn't just about loans and credit cards. It can shape your entire lifestyle. With a high score, you're not just saving money—you're giving yourself more freedom.

Better credit means better deals. From lower interest rates on mortgages to bigger credit card rewards, lenders *love* people with strong credit. That means your dream apartment is more accessible, your car payments are smaller, and you'll likely spend way less on interest over your lifetime. And hey, even some employers check credit as part of their hiring process—so keeping that score pretty can pay off in ways beyond your wallet.

But maybe the best flex? Knowing you're in control. In a world where it's easy to feel financially overwhelmed, a strong credit score is like holding the keys to your own kingdom. It's proof that you're managing your money on your terms—and that kind of confidence is priceless.

At the end of the day, building and maintaining good credit is less about perfection and more about consistency. You don't need to obsess over your score daily, but a little awareness goes a long way. Pay your bills on time, keep your balances low, and don't fall for quick-fix schemes.

And if your score isn't quite where you want it yet? That's okay. It's a marathon, not a sprint. Every smart move you make today pays off down the road, giving you access to bigger dreams and better opportunities.

Credit isn't just a number—it's a power move. So, own it.

23

Wealth, but Make it Generational

LET'S BE HONEST—WHEN MOST PEOPLE hear the word *wealth*, their minds go straight to yachts, designer wardrobes, and sprawling estates. But real wealth? It's quieter than that. It's having the freedom to make choices without checking your bank balance first. It's knowing you'll be okay if an emergency hits. And, if you're playing the long game, it's about making sure your financial glow-up lasts beyond just *your* lifetime.

Generational wealth—passing down assets, security, and financial wisdom—is the ultimate level-up. It's about creating a life where future you (and future *them*) can thrive. But for a lot of people, especially if you didn't grow up with trust funds and financial advisors on speed dial, building long-term wealth can feel like a fantasy reserved for someone else. Spoiler alert: it's not. With the right moves, you can be the one to break cycles, build a financial legacy, and still live your best life along the way.

If you didn't grow up surrounded by healthy financial habits, you know how easy it is to fall into patterns that keep you stuck. Maybe it's the "spend it while you have it" mentality, or the belief that saving is only for people who earn more. Maybe debt feels like a normal part of life because everyone around you is juggling bills. These patterns aren't just random—they're often passed down through generations like a worn-out family recipe.

Breaking free from these cycles starts with awareness. Take a long, honest look at the money habits you've inherited. Were you taught to save or to spend? Did conversations about money feel open, or were they secretive and stressful? Recognizing these patterns is the first step toward unlearning them. And once you do? You get to be the one who changes the story.

One of the most empowering things you can do is start rewriting the script for yourself—and those who come after you. It doesn't mean living like a monk or hoarding every penny. It means making intentional choices that protect your future self while dismantling the financial habits that no longer serve you.

Save for You—And Those Who Follow

When it comes to generational wealth, the first priority is always securing your own financial stability. You can't pour from an empty cup, and you definitely can't build a legacy if you're living paycheck to paycheck.

Start by establishing a solid financial foundation—an emergency fund that could cover 3-6 months of expenses is your best financial bestie. Once you've got that cushion in place, long-term savings and investments become the name of the game. Consider opening a high-yield savings account for short-term goals and using tax-advantaged accounts (like a retirement plan) for the big picture.

And here's where things get real—if you want to make an impact that lasts beyond your own lifetime, you need to think about what you're leaving behind. This doesn't mean setting up million-dollar trust funds. It could be as simple as starting a dedicated savings account for future generations or contributing to an investment fund that grows over time. The point is to create a system where the wealth you build doesn't just stop with you.

Not Just for the Ultra-Rich

Estate planning sounds like something people with private islands do, but it's actually one of the most practical moves you can make—no matter your income level. And no, you don't need a legal team to get started.

At its core, estate planning is simply about making sure your assets (money, property, even personal items) go where you want them to when you're no longer around. A simple will can cover the basics—who gets what, and who's responsible for making sure it happens. And if you've got young kids or dependents, a will lets you designate guardianship, which is a power move in itself.

If you want to take it a step further, consider setting up a trust. While it might sound complicated, a trust is just a legal arrangement where you transfer assets to be managed on behalf of your beneficiaries. Trusts can provide tax benefits, protect assets from creditors, and ensure your wealth is distributed exactly how you want. Plus, they skip the messy, time-consuming probate process.

And if you're worried this all sounds expensive, breathe easy—there are affordable online platforms that make creating a will or trust easier (and cheaper) than ever. The bottom line? Estate planning isn't about preparing for death. It's about protecting your life's work and making things easier for the people you love.

Legacy-Building in Real Time

Here's the thing about generational wealth: it's not just about the numbers in your bank account. It's also about the knowledge you pass down. Money can be spent, lost, or mismanaged—but financial literacy is the gift that keeps on giving.

Start normalizing money conversations with the people

closest to you. Whether it's teaching younger family members about saving or sharing your financial wins and lessons learned, transparency is key. These are the conversations that shape how future generations handle money.

Another practical way to build your legacy? Invest in things that outlive you. This could mean buying property, contributing to community causes, or supporting educational opportunities for the next generation. Wealth isn't just about cash—it's about creating opportunities and resources that keep giving long after you're gone.

And here's the best part: you don't have to wait until you're "rich" to start. Every choice you make today—whether it's starting an investment account, teaching someone how to budget, or documenting your wishes—plants seeds for a legacy that grows beyond your lifetime.

Generational wealth isn't reserved for the lucky few. It's something you can build—one smart move at a time. By breaking free from toxic money cycles, prioritizing your own financial health, and making intentional choices for the future, you become the architect of a legacy that lasts.

And here's the truth—building generational wealth doesn't mean sacrificing the life you want to live right now. You can have both. You can prioritize joy while making future-proof decisions. You can splurge on what matters while stacking your financial security. You can live your best life while making sure the people you love are taken care of, too.

It's not about leaving millions behind. It's about leaving a roadmap. And every choice you make today is a step toward that bigger, brighter future.

24

Your Rich Person Era (It's Coming)

LET'S GET ONE THING STRAIGHT—YOUR rich person era isn't some distant, unattainable dream reserved for trust fund babies and crypto bros. It's not about manifesting piles of cash by scribbling affirmations in a journal (though, hey, no judgment if that's your thing). Real wealth—the kind that sticks—is built on habits, not luck. It's about making consistent, intentional choices that set you up for a life where money isn't a constant stressor. And the best part? You don't have to wait until retirement to feel the effects.

If you're playing the long game, your rich person era isn't a maybe—it's inevitable. But building and keeping wealth isn't just about earning more. It's about future-proofing your finances, cultivating habits that actually last, and designing a lifestyle you won't outgrow when your bank balance starts reflecting your glow-up. Because let's be honest—what's the point of building wealth if you're too burned out to enjoy it?

The Power of Boring (a.k.a. Wealth's Best-Kept Secret)

Here's the truth nobody puts on a vision board: lasting wealth is pretty boring. There are no viral hacks or overnight shortcuts.

It's compound interest quietly working its magic. It's automating savings so you don't have to think about it. It's making smart decisions when nobody's watching—like skipping that impulse purchase and putting the money toward something that actually matters.

But don't mistake "boring" for "hard." The small habits that lead to real wealth are surprisingly simple when you break them down. Automating your savings and investments means you're building wealth on autopilot. Keeping your lifestyle creep in check ensures you're not blowing every raise on things you didn't actually need when you were making less. And living below your means—without living like you're in a financial straitjacket—is where the magic happens.

Think of it like planting a money tree. At first, it feels slow. There's no instant gratification. But the longer you let those habits grow, the more your wealth multiplies—and suddenly, you're the one with financial freedom while everyone else is still grinding.

Future-Proofing Your Money Moves

Let's talk about future-proofing—because nothing kills a rich person era faster than a financial blind spot. Unexpected emergencies, market dips, and even your own future desires can derail your financial progress if you're not prepared.

Start by protecting your current and future self. That means having an emergency fund—yes, still—because even when you're rolling in cash, life loves to throw curveballs. Aim for 6 to 12 months' worth of expenses if you want real peace of mind.

And then there's insurance. Not the sexiest topic, but vital if you want to stay wealthy. Health, disability, and life insurance might feel unnecessary when you're thriving, but they're the safety net that keeps everything intact when things go sideways.

Investments are another key piece of the future-proofing puzzle. It's not enough to stash your money in a savings account and hope for the best. Long-term wealth grows when your money works harder than you do. And no, you don't need to become a stock market guru—index funds and diversified portfolios can do the heavy lifting while you live your life.

But future-proofing isn't just about defense. It's also about setting yourself up for the dreams you haven't even dreamed yet. Want to take a year off and travel? Buy property? Start a passion project? That future you is counting on the choices you make today.

How to Stay Rich (Without Becoming a Miser)

Getting rich is one thing—staying rich is a whole other game. And here's the kicker: most people lose wealth not because they stop making money, but because they stop managing it.

The secret to maintaining wealth is balance. You don't need to hoard every penny in the name of "security," but you also can't treat every paycheck like Monopoly money. Smart spending isn't about depriving yourself—it's about spending in alignment with your values.

That means curating your "rich person" lifestyle around what genuinely makes you happy, not just what looks good on Instagram. Maybe it's a beautiful home where you feel safe and comfortable. Maybe it's the freedom to travel or the ability to support causes you care about. Whatever it is, your money should enhance your life—not control it.

And while you're building your empire, don't forget to keep learning. The financial world evolves, and staying wealthy means staying curious. Keep an eye on new investment opportunities, tax strategies, and lifestyle tweaks that help you protect and grow what you've built.

Designing a Life You Won't Outgrow

Here's the thing no one tells you about the "rich life"—if you're not intentional, it's easy to build a life that doesn't even fit you. You can accumulate all the stuff, status, and success markers, only to realize they don't bring the happiness you thought they would.

The antidote? Build a life that feels like *you*—not the version of yourself you think you should be. What does your ideal day look like? Who are you spending time with? What experiences feel truly meaningful? These are the questions that shape a lifestyle you won't outgrow, no matter how much your bank balance evolves.

And don't be afraid to adjust. Wealth is a tool—not a destination. If your priorities shift, your financial habits should shift with them. Whether it's downsizing to make space for freedom or scaling up to support new goals, your money should always be working toward a life you genuinely love.

Here's the bottom line: your rich person era isn't some future version of you living in a mansion—it's the choices you make today, stacking up quietly in the background. It's the automated savings you barely think about. The investments working for you while you sleep. The intentional choices to spend, save, and give in ways that align with who you are.

You're already on your way. And the best part? You don't have to wait until you hit a magic number to start living like it. Your rich person era is coming—but if you look closely, you'll realize it's already here.

PART 6

Living Richer, Spending Smarter

25

The Luxe-for-Less Lifestyle

LIVING A LUXURIOUS LIFE DOESN'T have to come with a sky-high price tag. Forget the myth that opulence is reserved for those with unlimited bank balances—because, in reality, luxury is more about how you curate your life than how much you spend. The real flex isn't maxing out your credit card on designer labels or splurging on a five-star vacation you can barely afford—it's knowing how to enjoy the finer things without waking up to a zero balance.

The truth is, luxury isn't just about the price—it's about the feeling. And when you start defining what luxury means to *you*, rather than what it looks like on social media, you unlock a lifestyle that feels just as indulgent—without the financial hangover. You don't need to spend like a billionaire to live richly; you just need to know when to splurge, when to save, and how to get the best of both worlds.

The basic rule is you need to know when to fake it, when to splurge. Not everything needs to be "the real deal." In fact, the art of living luxuriously on a budget is knowing when to invest and when to cut corners—without losing the aesthetic (or the experience). The secret? Prioritize the things you touch, wear, or experience every day.

For example, splurging on high-quality basics—like a well-tailored blazer or a luxe pair of everyday shoes—pays off because they elevate your wardrobe and last longer. But trendy items? Those can absolutely be faked. Fast fashion is your friend when it comes to seasonal styles that'll be out of rotation by next year. And no, you don't need to buy a $3,000 designer bag to exude "quiet luxury"—a sleek, well-made dupe can deliver the same vibe for a fraction of the price.

The same rule applies to experiences. If you're craving a high-end spa day but your wallet says no, recreate the vibe at home. Fancy candle? Check. Plush robe? Check. A few indulgent skincare products? Done. You get the relaxation and luxury without dropping a small fortune. But when it comes to moments that truly matter—like a once-in-a-lifetime vacation or a dinner at a Michelin-starred restaurant—it's worth splurging if the experience is meaningful to you.

The trick is simple: spend on what you'll treasure, save on what you'll forget.

Luxury Isn't Always What It Looks Like

We live in a world where "luxury" is often sold as something you can buy—a designer label, an exotic vacation, a pristine minimalist home. But real luxury? It's more personal than price tags. Sometimes, luxury is waking up without an alarm clock. It's having the time to meet friends for an unhurried coffee. It's the freedom to book a spontaneous weekend trip because your finances aren't hanging by a thread.

Reframing luxury starts by asking yourself: *What feels indulgent to me?* Maybe it's ordering your favourite dessert without overthinking the cost. Maybe it's paying for a cleaner because you value your time more than scrubbing floors. Maybe it's investing in a cozy, beautiful home because you crave a sanctuary. When you define luxury on your own terms, you stop chasing what looks impressive and start curating what actually brings you joy.

And here's the real flex: living well without broadcasting it. The quiet luxury lifestyle isn't about showing off—it's about crafting a life where comfort, beauty, and ease are built into your daily routine. No logos required.

The Luxe-for-Less Playbook

So, how do you actually live a luxe life on a realistic budget? It's part strategy, part mindset shift. You don't have to overhaul your life or cut out indulgences completely—you just need to be intentional about where your money goes.

1. **Shop Smart, Not Fast:** The fastest way to waste money? Impulse buying. The smartest way to save? Being a savvy shopper. Wait for sales, scout luxury consignment stores, and use cashback apps to score high-end items for less. Designer bags, vintage furniture, and even luxury beauty products can be found for a steal if you know where to look. And when you do splurge, think long-term—invest in timeless pieces over fleeting trends.
2. **Master the Art of Dupes:** Why spend a fortune when the high-quality dupe does the job? From beauty products to home décor, there are plenty of brands delivering designer-quality without the luxury markup. You'd be surprised how many influencers flaunting luxury are actually wearing affordable alternatives—because the look matters more than the label.
3. **Prioritize Experiences Over Things:** Luxury isn't always a thing you own—it's a feeling you cultivate. A beautifully plated meal, a scenic road trip, a cozy weekend retreat—these experiences offer a richer sense of luxury than any logo-laden

accessory ever could. Invest in memories, not just material things.
4. **Curate, Don't Consume:** True luxury lies in having fewer, better things. Instead of filling your space (and life) with cheap, disposable items, focus on curating a collection of things you genuinely love. It's not about having a closet stuffed with designer labels—it's about having a wardrobe where every piece makes you feel your best.
5. **Craft Your Own Luxury Rituals:** You don't need to spend a fortune to infuse everyday life with a touch of luxury. Light a fancy candle on an ordinary Tuesday. Use the nice wine glasses—even if it's for soda. Turn your morning skincare routine into a spa-like ritual. Small upgrades to your daily habits can transform even the most basic routines into moments of indulgence.

The ultimate luxury is choice—the freedom to design a life that feels rich in every way. It's not about how much you spend; it's about how intentional you are with your money. And when you start aligning your spending with what actually matters to you, you realize you don't need to be a millionaire to live like one.

So, if you're craving the luxe life, start by defining it for yourself. Spend where it counts. Save where it doesn't. And remember: the most luxurious thing you can own is peace of mind—and that's always within reach.

26

Save Without the Sacrifice

SAVING MONEY OFTEN FEELS LIKE a tug-of-war between two opposing forces—your financial goals and the life you actually want to live. Somewhere between the endless advice to cut lattes and the guilt-ridden reminders to "just save more," the whole idea of building a savings cushion can start to feel like punishment. But here's the truth: saving doesn't have to mean stripping your life of all joy. In fact, when done right, saving becomes less about deprivation and more about freedom—the freedom to make choices without financial panic lurking in the background.

The trick isn't to overhaul your entire lifestyle overnight or guilt yourself into cutting every "unnecessary" expense. Instead, it's about weaving saving into your daily life in a way that feels easy and automatic—without making you feel like you're living under a financial dictatorship. When saving becomes part of your rhythm, you get the best of both worlds: a growing bank balance and a life you still enjoy.

Why Saving Feels Like a Struggle (and How to Change That)

Saving doesn't come naturally for most people. Between the allure of instant gratification and the way modern life normalizes spending at every turn, stashing money away feels like swimming upstream. Add in the mental gymnastics of "I deserve to treat myself" and the pressure to keep up with everyone else's highlight reel, and it's no wonder saving often feels like punishment.

But here's the reframe: saving isn't about saying "no" to everything fun—it's about creating options. It's the difference between being trapped by your next paycheck and having the freedom to make moves that serve *you*. When you approach saving from a place of empowerment instead of restriction, it becomes easier to make choices that align with both your current happiness and your future security.

One of the biggest mental blocks around saving is the idea that you have to suffer to do it—that every penny saved comes at the expense of joy. This isn't just unhelpful; it's unsustainable. Long-term saving only works when it feels integrated, not imposed. It's about shifting from a scarcity mindset (where saving means losing out) to an abundance mindset (where saving creates more freedom).

Automating Good Money Habits—Because Willpower Isn't Enough

If you're relying on willpower alone to save, you're fighting a losing battle. Life is full of tempting "buy now" moments, and no matter how disciplined you are, manual saving eventually falls through the cracks. The solution? Automate it.

Automating your savings removes the decision fatigue and makes the process feel effortless. The money moves itself before you even have a chance to miss it. Set up a system where a portion of your paycheck goes directly into a savings account. Better yet, have multiple savings buckets—one for emergencies, one for short-term goals, and one for guilt-free splurges. By separating your money upfront, you're protecting your future self without constantly debating whether you should transfer that extra $50.

And here's a secret: you don't need to start big for automation to work. Even small amounts—£10 here, £20 there—add up over time. The key is consistency. When saving happens automatically, you're building a financial buffer without having to think about it, making it easier to stick to your goals while still enjoying life in the present.

Drop the Financial Guilt Trips

We've all been there—spending on something fun only to feel a wave of guilt after. Society loves to shame people for spending money on "frivolous" things (hello, latte-shaming culture), but here's the thing: your budget doesn't need to be a prison. The goal isn't to cut everything enjoyable—it's to save in a way that reflects what *you* value.

The best way to ditch the guilt is to get intentional about your spending. Identify your "non-negotiables"—the things that bring you genuine joy—and make room for them in your budget without apology. Maybe it's your twice-monthly massage, your favourite streaming service, or spontaneous weekend getaways. When you prioritize what actually matters to you, you naturally spend less on things that don't.

Guilt-free saving is about striking a balance. You can enjoy life now while still preparing for the future. It's not an either-or scenario. The trick is creating a plan that allows both—because let's face it, joyless saving isn't sustainable, and neither is reckless spending. The sweet spot lies in mindful money management: knowing when to indulge, when to hold back, and when to unapologetically say, "Yes, I'm saving for future me—but I'm also living for today."

Finding Freedom Through Mindful Spending

Mindful spending isn't about penny-pinching—it's about spending on purpose. It's asking yourself, *Is this purchase aligned with my values, goals, and lifestyle?* Instead of defaulting to autopilot spending (scroll, click, buy), it's about making intentional choices that reflect what you genuinely care about.

Start by tracking your spending—not to shame yourself, but to get clear on where your money actually goes. You might discover patterns you didn't expect. Maybe you're spending more on impulse delivery orders than you realize, or maybe those subscription fees are quietly stacking up. Knowing where your money flows gives you the power to redirect it toward what really matters.

And here's a powerful mindset shift: Every pound you save isn't just money—it's freedom. It's the ability to quit a soul-sucking job, take an impromptu trip, or say "yes" to unexpected opportunities. The more you save, the more options you create for your future self.

The biggest secret to saving without the sacrifice? Design a system that works *with* your lifestyle, not against it. Instead of focusing on what you're cutting, focus on what you're creating—more freedom, more security, more peace of mind. Saving isn't the enemy of fun; it's the thing that lets you enjoy life without fear.

By automating smart habits, ditching the guilt, and spending with intention, you can save without sacrificing the life you love. And when saving becomes second nature, you're not just building a healthier bank balance—you're building a future where your money works for you, not the other way around.

27

Boundaries, but Make Them Financial

MONEY MAY NOT BE THE root of all evil, but it sure knows how to stir up drama—especially when it comes to the people closest to you. From the friend who always "forgets" their wallet to the family member with a never-ending list of financial favours, navigating money conversations can feel like walking a tightrope. And let's be real—setting financial boundaries isn't exactly a hot topic at brunch. But here's the thing: without clear money boundaries, your bank account becomes a free-for-all, and your peace of mind takes the hit.

Financial boundaries aren't just about saying "no" to requests—they're about protecting your financial well-being while preserving your relationships. Because if you're constantly bending your budget to keep the peace, you're not just losing money—you're losing control. The good news? You can draw the line without turning into a villain. It's all about clarity, confidence, and knowing that setting limits doesn't make you selfish—it makes you smart.

Why Financial Boundaries Feel So Uncomfortable

Money is tangled up with emotion. It's not just currency—it's love, power, obligation, and sometimes, guilt. So, when someone you care about asks for financial help, saying "no" feels like rejecting the person, not just the request. And society doesn't make it easier—there's an unspoken rule that says if you *can* help, you *should*. This emotional tug-of-war is why so many people drain their savings or stretch beyond their means just to avoid an awkward conversation.

But here's the hard truth: your financial health is your responsibility. No one else is going to prioritize your goals the way you will. If you keep letting others' needs take priority, you're silently saying your own future doesn't matter as much. And that's not fair—to you *or* to them. Setting financial boundaries isn't about being cold-hearted; it's about recognizing that your long-term stability deserves protection.

The first step to reclaiming control? Let go of the guilt. You can be generous *and* have limits. You can care deeply about people without becoming their personal ATM. And here's the kicker: when you enforce healthy boundaries, you're modeling something powerful—how to value yourself and your financial future.

How to Set—and Stick to—Financial Boundaries

Let's be clear: boundaries don't work unless they're enforced. And while it's easy to say, "I'm not lending money anymore," it's a whole different game when a loved one is in tears asking for help. So, how do you set boundaries that actually hold up under pressure? It starts with knowing your limits—and being ready to communicate them clearly.

Not all boundaries look the same. Maybe you're fine picking up a casual dinner tab but draw the line at co-signing a loan. Or perhaps you're open to one-time gifts but refuse to become someone's ongoing financial safety net. Take time to map out your personal "yes," "no," and "maybe" zones. Knowing your boundaries in advance makes it easier to stand firm when the moment arises.

Think of this as your financial "terms and conditions." Decide in advance how much you're willing to give (and to whom). Maybe you set a yearly cap on financial gifts, or you only contribute to emergencies, not lifestyle expenses. Having a personal policy takes the emotional guesswork out of requests. When you know your own rules, there's no need to waffle or feel guilty when you say "no."

Awkward money conversations are inevitable, but they don't have to catch you off guard. Having a few go-to scripts in your back pocket makes it easier to enforce your boundaries without scrambling for words. A simple, "I'd love to help, but I'm focused on my financial goals right now," can shut down a request while keeping the conversation respectful. And if someone keeps pushing? That's a them problem—not a you problem.

What to Say When the Answer is No

Saying "no" doesn't have to be cold or harsh. You can decline with kindness while still holding firm. Here are a few ways to gracefully set financial boundaries without burning bridges:

For Friends Who Expect You to Split Big Bills:
"I love hanging out with you, but I'm keeping a tighter budget right now. Let's find a place that works for both of us!"
For Family Members Who Keep Asking for Loans:
"I wish I could help, but I've made a rule for myself not to lend money to anyone."
For Someone Who Keeps Pushing:
"I understand where you're coming from, but I have to stick to my financial priorities right now. I hope you understand."

The key? Be kind, be clear, and don't apologize for protecting your future.

When Helping Hurts: Knowing Your Limits

There's a fine line between generosity and self-sacrifice. And while it's noble to want to support your loved ones, there's no prize for draining yourself dry. Before you say "yes" to any financial request, ask yourself:

> *Can I afford to give this without jeopardizing my own goals?*
> *Is this a one-time situation, or am I enabling a pattern?*
> *Would they do the same for me if the roles were reversed?*

If the answer to any of these is "no," it's a sign that setting (or reinforcing) a boundary is necessary. Because here's the truth: real love isn't about how much you give—it's about mutual respect. And if someone can't respect your financial boundaries, it's time to reevaluate that dynamic.

When Saying "Yes" Makes Sense

Not every financial request is a red flag. Sometimes, helping someone out is a meaningful and positive choice—as long as it's done on your terms. If you do choose to say "yes," set clear expectations. Is this a gift or a loan? If it's a loan, what are the repayment terms? And most importantly, only give what you can truly afford to lose—because even the best intentions can go sideways.

Financial boundaries are an act of self-care. They protect your savings, your mental health, and your future. And while enforcing them can feel uncomfortable at first, it gets easier with practice. The more you honor your limits, the more empowered you become.

At the end of the day, you don't owe anyone access to your wallet. Your money is a reflection of your time, energy, and hard work—and you get to decide how you use it. By setting financial boundaries, you're not just safeguarding your savings—you're reclaiming your power and giving yourself the freedom to build the life *you* want. And that? That's priceless.

28

Spending With Purpose

MONEY TALKS—BUT WHAT IS YOURS saying about you? In a world where spending is often impulsive and fueled by trends, aligning your money with your values can feel like a radical act. It's easy to swipe without thinking, to let your cash flow toward things that bring temporary pleasure but little long-term satisfaction. But when you start spending with intention—when your purchases reflect your priorities—money becomes more than just a transaction. It becomes a tool for building a life that actually feels good.

Spending with purpose doesn't mean living on a shoestring or cutting out the things you love. It's not about guilt-tripping yourself for wanting nice things or treating yourself. Instead, it's about becoming conscious of where your money goes and making sure it supports the life you want to create. When you shift from mindless consumption to intentional spending, every dollar becomes a reflection of what truly matters to you. And that's when money stops feeling like a source of stress—and starts feeling like freedom.

Let's be honest—mindless spending is *fun*. The thrill of a new purchase, the rush of a good deal, the ease of clicking "buy now"—it's all designed to keep you spending without thinking too much. And the modern world doesn't exactly encourage mindfulness. Targeted ads, influencer culture, and the endless scroll of "must-haves" make it ridiculously easy to spend without considering whether it actually serves you.

But here's the thing: while those impulse buys might deliver a temporary dopamine hit, they rarely lead to lasting happiness. In fact, the more we spend without intention, the more disconnected we become from our real desires. That's how people end up surrounded by stuff but still feeling unfulfilled—because spending without purpose doesn't nourish the things that actually matter.

So how do you shift from impulse to intention? It starts with asking yourself a simple but powerful question: *Why am I spending this money?*

Spending That Aligns With Your Values

When you align your spending with your values, your purchases become a reflection of who you are and what you stand for. But to do that, you first need to know what those values are. What matters most to you? Is it freedom? Security? Adventure? Creativity? Your spending should fuel those priorities—not work against them.

For instance:

If freedom is your value, prioritizing savings and experiences over material things might feel more aligned.

If community is important to you, investing in local businesses or supporting causes you care about could be a spending priority.

If personal growth matters most, you might choose to spend on education, books, or therapy rather than fleeting luxuries.

The point isn't to judge your spending—it's to make sure your money reflects your values. Because when you spend in alignment with what you care about, every dollar starts to feel more meaningful.

The Joy of Conscious Spending

Here's a secret no one tells you: intentional spending doesn't feel restrictive—it feels empowering. When you start spending on things that genuinely align with your values, you don't feel deprived. You feel in control.

Think about the purchases you've made that bring you real joy. Maybe it's the solo trip you saved for, the kitchen gadget that makes your mornings easier, or the donation you made to a cause close to your heart. Those are the kinds of purchases that deliver a deeper, more lasting satisfaction. And the more you practice conscious spending, the easier it becomes to distinguish between what's meaningful and what's just noise.

Of course, this doesn't mean you can't buy things purely for fun. The key is to be intentional. Ask yourself: *Does this bring real value to my life? Will I still care about this purchase a month from now?* If the answer is no, maybe that money is better spent elsewhere—or saved for something that will actually matter in the long run.

How to Spend with Purpose (Without Killing Your Vibe)

Spending with intention doesn't mean you have to scrutinize every latte or give up spontaneous joy. It's not about rigid rules—it's about making choices that serve you instead of draining you. Here are some ways to get started:

What's genuinely worth spending on? Identify the categories where you want to spend freely—whether it's travel, fitness, quality food, or gifts for loved ones. These are your financial priorities. By getting clear on what matters most, you can cut back on the things that don't and invest more in what brings you happiness.

Take a no-judgment look at your recent purchases. Which ones still bring you joy? Which ones feel like a waste? Recognizing these patterns can help you make more intentional choices moving forward.

Impulse buys lose their power when you press "pause." Before making a purchase, give yourself time to think it through. Ask: *Is this aligned with my values? Is it adding something meaningful to my life?* If not, it's probably not worth it.

Research shows that people get more long-term happiness from experiences than from material goods. Prioritize spending on things that create memories—like travel, hobbies, or quality time with loved ones.

Your values and goals will evolve over time, so make it a habit to review and adjust your spending. What felt important last year might not align with where you are now. Stay flexible and give yourself permission to shift your spending accordingly.

Intentional spending isn't about deprivation—it's about freedom. It's about making your money work *for* you, instead of letting it control you. And the best part? When your spending reflects your values, you don't just feel richer—you feel more aligned, more in control, and more at peace with where your money is going.

So, the next time you're about to tap your card or click "buy," pause. Ask yourself: *Is this supporting the life I want to build?* If the answer is yes—go for it. But if it's not? Let it go. Because the ultimate flex isn't just spending—it's spending with purpose.

PART 7

Mastering Everyday Money Moves

29

The Lazy Guide to Saving

SAVING MONEY GETS A BAD reputation. It's often framed as a discipline-heavy, spreadsheet-filled grind where you have to scrutinize every expense and track every penny. But here's a reality check—saving doesn't have to be exhausting. In fact, the lazier you make it, the more likely you are to stick with it. It's not about willpower; it's about setting things up so that saving happens in the background while you live your life. Think of it as the financial equivalent of "set it and forget it." No complicated budgets. No hours spent pouring over receipts. Just small, consistent moves that make saving effortless.

Most people fail to save because they overcomplicate it. They think they need a perfectly optimized budget, a deep understanding of investment portfolios, or the discipline of a monk. But the truth? Saving is easier when you get out of your own way. If you build simple, low-effort systems that work automatically, you'll stack cash without even thinking about it. And when saving feels easy, it stops being a chore—and starts becoming a habit you barely notice.

Why Lazy Saving Works (and Why Willpower Doesn't)

Relying on willpower to save money is like relying on motivation to hit the gym—it works for a while, but eventually, life gets in the way. When saving requires constant effort, it's easy to let it slide the minute things get busy. That's why the lazy approach is smarter. It's about building systems that do the heavy lifting for you, so your future self is taken care of without needing to make daily decisions.

Automation is your best friend here. When saving happens automatically, you remove the temptation to spend first and save later. And let's be real—that "I'll save whatever's left at the end of the month" strategy rarely works. If the money is sitting in your checking account, it's basically already gone. The trick is to move your savings out of sight before you even notice it's there.

Lazy saving isn't about doing nothing—it's about doing *less* while getting *more* results. Small, automatic moves add up over time, and when you make saving easy, you stop stressing about it. So, instead of relying on sheer willpower, let's make saving as effortless as scrolling through your phone.

Step 1: Automate It and Forget It

If you do nothing else, automate your savings. This is the golden rule of lazy saving. When you set up automatic transfers, money moves itself into your savings without you lifting a finger. You don't have to remember. You don't have to think about it. It just happens.

Here's the play:

Split Your Paycheck: Set up a direct deposit that sends a portion of your income straight to a separate savings account. Even 5-10% is a solid start.

Recurring Transfers: Schedule a monthly or weekly transfer from your checking account to your savings. The smaller the amount, the less you'll feel it.

Round-Up Apps: Use apps that round up your purchases to the nearest dollar and save the spare change. It's like throwing your digital coins into a jar—but easier.

Automation takes the decision-making out of saving, which means you save consistently without even realizing it. And the best part? You can start small. Even $10 a week adds up over time—without impacting your day-to-day spending.

Step 2: Micro-Saving Hacks for Minimal Effort

If automating your savings is the lazy gold standard, micro-saving is its low-key sidekick. These are the small, painless moves that build your savings in the background. No spreadsheets. No complicated tracking. Just tiny shifts that compound over time.

Here are some easy micro-saving moves that require zero mental energy:

The "Invisible Raise" Trick: Every time you get a raise, bonus, or unexpected cash, increase your automatic savings. You won't miss the money because you never got used to spending it.

The $5 Rule: Every time you get a $5 bill (or any small denomination), set it aside. If you want to keep it digital, transfer $5 to your savings account every time you treat yourself to something fun.

"No-Spend Day" Rewards: For every day you don't spend on non-essentials, transfer a small amount—like $2 or $5—into savings. It turns saving into a game without major sacrifice.

Subscription Sweeps: Cancel unused subscriptions and redirect those payments straight into your savings. It's money you were already spending, so you won't feel the pinch.

The key to micro-saving is consistency, not size. Small amounts add up fast when you do them consistently—and because these moves are painless, they fit easily into your daily routine.

Step 3: Low-Effort Tracking (Without the Spreadsheet)

Let's face it—no one wants to spend their free time categorizing every coffee purchase. Traditional budgeting is time-consuming and, for most people, unsustainable. But if you want to save effortlessly, it helps to have a sense of where your money is going. The lazy solution? Automate your tracking.

Here's how to keep tabs on your money without a headache:

Use Auto-Tracking Apps: Apps like Mint, YNAB, or your bank's built-in tools automatically track your spending. Set it up once, and let the app do the work.

Check-In, Don't Obsess: Instead of a daily audit, do a quick weekly or monthly check-in. Are you hitting your savings goals? Are you overspending in one area? Small adjustments go a long way.

Set Spending Alerts: Many banks let you set alerts when you're close to hitting a spending limit. It's like having a financial guardrail that nudges you before you go overboard.

The goal isn't perfection—it's awareness. When you know where your money is going, you can make smarter choices without micromanaging every dollar.

Step 4: Make It Fun (Because Saving Doesn't Have to Suck)

Saving gets easier when you make it feel good. Instead of treating it like a chore, turn it into a game. Celebrate your milestones. Set fun incentives. Trick your brain into thinking saving is a win—not a loss.

Try these lazy-friendly motivation hacks:

Take on a no-spend weekend or a $100 savings sprint. Small,

time-limited challenges keep things interesting without feeling overwhelming.

Use a savings jar, a digital goal tracker, or even a sticky note chart. Seeing your progress in real-time makes saving feel rewarding.

When you hit a savings milestone, treat yourself—just don't undo your progress.

Saving isn't just about the future—it's about feeling empowered now. And when you make it easy and fun, it stops feeling like a grind and starts feeling like a flex.

Lazy Saving = Smarter Saving

The truth is, saving doesn't have to be hard—it just has to be automatic. By setting up simple systems that work in the background, you remove the mental load and make saving part of your daily life.

You don't need to overhaul your entire financial system overnight. Start small. Automate a little. Add micro-savings where you can. And before you know it, you'll be stacking cash without even trying. Because the best way to save isn't through willpower—it's through building a lazy, effortless system that works while you live your life.

And honestly? That's the kind of lazy we can all get behind.

30

Cash Flow, But Make It Sexy

CASH FLOW—THE UNSEXY BACKBONE OF financial stability. It's the money coming in and going out of your life, dictating whether you feel financially free or forever one bad month away from a meltdown. While it might not sound glamorous, mastering your cash flow is like having VIP access to the life you actually want. When you control your cash flow, you control your choices. And when you smooth out the bumps, you stop living paycheck to paycheck and start feeling like the main character in your financial story.

But here's the thing—most people don't think about cash flow until there's a problem. You know the feeling: it's the middle of the month, your rent is due, your social calendar is popping off, and somehow your bank account is already whispering, *"Girl, please."* This isn't just about budgeting—it's about understanding how to keep your money moving in a way that supports your life without constantly feeling broke. So, let's break down how to make your cash flow work for you—without the financial jargon or the guilt trips.

Where the Money Actually Goes (And Why It Feels Like It Disappears)

Ever wonder how your paycheck evaporates so fast? You're not alone. The truth is, most of us have no idea where our money actually goes—until it's gone. Sure, you remember the big stuff like rent and groceries, but it's the sneaky, everyday spending that drains your cash flow faster than you realize.

Here's the reality: cash flow problems rarely come from one massive splurge. It's the accumulation of little, seemingly harmless purchases—the random coffee runs, last-minute Ubers, and those "just one thing" Target trips that always turn into a cart full of stuff. On paper, you're earning enough. But in practice? Your money is slipping through your fingers, and the cycle feels impossible to break.

The first step to sexier cash flow? Awareness. And no, this doesn't mean tracking every single penny (because who has time for that?). It's about identifying your "money leaks"—those expenses that quietly drain your cash without adding real value to your life. Once you know where your cash is going, you can start making intentional moves to keep more of it.

Smoothing Out Money Droughts (No More Mid-Month Panic)

The ultimate cash flow fantasy is a life where money feels consistent—no matter what's happening in your bank account. But for most people, cash flow feels more like a rollercoaster. Some weeks, you're living large. Others? You're wondering if air counts as a meal. This feast-or-famine cycle isn't just stressful—it's unsustainable.

The secret to smoothing out those "money droughts" is to ditch the chaotic, reactive approach to your finances. Instead of spending freely when you're flush and clenching your wallet when you're broke, aim for consistency. This means spreading out your expenses and creating a system where your cash flow feels steady, even when life throws you curveballs.

Here's a move that works like magic: timing your bills to match your paycheck schedule. If you get paid twice a month, split your major expenses between those paychecks—rent on one, utilities and groceries on the other. If your bills are due all at once, call your service providers and ask to shift due dates. Most companies are weirdly flexible if you just ask.

Another hack? Create your own "buffer account." This is a small stash of cash (think $300–$500) that you park in a separate account and use to cover any shortfalls between paydays. It's like financial floaties—keeping you afloat during low-cash moments without dipping into your emergency fund.

Stretching Your Paycheck (Without Feeling Deprived)

Making your paycheck last longer isn't about cutting out all joy—it's about spending smarter so you feel satisfied without draining your account. The key is to create a spending rhythm that fits your lifestyle while protecting your cash flow.

One game-changer? The "Pay Yourself First" method. Before you pay bills, buy groceries, or even breathe, move a set amount to savings. This flips the usual script of saving whatever's "leftover" (which, let's be real, is usually nothing). Automating this step ensures that you're building financial security while still enjoying your life.

And if you want your paycheck to stretch even further, plan your splurges in advance. Spontaneous spending feels fun in the moment but burns through cash fast. Instead, give yourself a "fun money" budget each month—a guilt-free amount you can blow on whatever you want. Knowing you have designated spending cash makes it easier to say no to impulse buys.

Finally, pace your spending. Most people blow through their

paycheck in the first two weeks, leaving the rest of the month feeling like a financial wasteland. Instead of front-loading all your spending, break it into weekly chunks. If you have $600 for non-essentials, divide it into $150 per week. This keeps you from overindulging early and suffering later.

Keeping Your Cash Flow Positive (Without Hustling Harder)

A positive cash flow—where you consistently bring in more than you spend—is the holy grail of financial freedom. But the answer isn't always "earn more." Yes, more income helps, but the real game is managing what you already have.

One easy win? Cutting "lazy leaks." These are expenses you're paying for out of habit, not necessity. Subscriptions you forgot about. Premium memberships you never use. That gym membership you "plan" to use next month (but haven't touched in six). Scrubbing these unnecessary costs instantly frees up cash without affecting your lifestyle.

And if you want to boost your cash flow without burning yourself out, monetize what you already do. If you love photography, offer casual photo sessions. Obsessed with organizing? Sell your services to friends who can't manage their closets. You don't need to launch a full-blown side hustle—just find small, easy ways to turn your talents into extra cash.

Another power move? Revisit your fixed expenses annually. Car insurance, phone plans, and internet bills aren't set in stone. Companies quietly raise rates over time, but a quick call to negotiate—or switching to a competitor—can shave hundreds off your annual costs.

When your cash flow works, everything else gets easier. You're not stuck in a cycle of panic and restriction. You're in control. You can afford what matters. You're free to say "yes" to opportunities without worrying if your bank account can keep up.

And here's the truth—financial confidence is a whole vibe. It's knowing that your money is working for you, not against you. It's feeling empowered to make choices from a place of abundance, not fear. When you master your cash flow, you're not just managing money—you're curating a life that feels rich in every sense of the word.

So, go ahead. Make your cash flow sexy. Keep it smooth, consistent, and effortless—because there's nothing hotter than knowing your money game is strong.

31

When Fun Has a Price Tag

FUN IS RARELY FREE—AT LEAST, not the kind you actually want. Spontaneous weekend getaways, bottomless brunches, concert tickets, and nights out with friends all come with a price tag that can quietly drain your bank account if you're not paying attention. But here's the thing—cutting out fun entirely isn't the answer. Life's too short to say no to joy just because you're chasing financial goals. The real flex? Learning how to indulge in the things you love without waking up to a financial hangover.

The problem isn't having fun—it's the way fun often sneaks up on you. You're invited to an impromptu dinner, and suddenly that "quick bite" turns into a three-course feast with craft cocktails. A friend suggests a weekend trip, and before you know it, your credit card is carrying the burden of spontaneous travel costs. Fun is seductive that way—it whispers, *"You deserve this,"* while your bank account side-eyes you in the background.

The truth is, you don't have to choose between enjoying your life and protecting your finances. The key is to treat fun like any other essential expense—something you intentionally budget for, rather than an afterthought. When you give your joy a financial place of honor, it stops being the thing that derails your goals and becomes part of a balanced, satisfying life.

The Myth of "Irresponsible Fun"

Somewhere along the way, we learned that being financially responsible meant being boring. Canceling plans, avoiding splurges, and turning down every invitation that costs money. But here's the twist—cutting out fun isn't the fast track to wealth; it's a shortcut to burnout. Because eventually, deprivation backfires. When you deny yourself joy for too long, those little indulgences turn into full-blown spending binges.

Think about the last time you "rewarded" yourself for being responsible. Maybe you spent a quiet month at home, avoiding all non-essential expenses. Then, out of nowhere, you snapped—impulse-booked a weekend trip, splurged on designer shoes, or treated yourself to a "just because" shopping spree. This isn't a lack of discipline—it's your brain rebelling against scarcity. And unless you plan for joy, that rebellion will keep repeating itself.

The solution? Make fun a non-negotiable line in your budget. When you treat fun like a bill you owe yourself, you remove the guilt. It becomes something you prioritize—not something that sneaks up on you and derails your financial progress.

Budgeting for Joy

Here's where most people go wrong—they think budgeting for fun means limiting it. But it's not about cutting out joy; it's about making space for it. Think of it as building a "fun fund" specifically for the experiences and indulgences that light you up.

Start by asking yourself: *What does fun look like for me?* For some, it's spontaneous dinners and live shows. For others, it's regular self-care rituals or weekend getaways. The goal is to align your spending with the things that genuinely bring you joy—not the things you do out of obligation or FOMO.

Once you know your version of fun, **assign it a number.** Maybe that's $100 a month for little indulgences or $500 for a quarterly splurge. The magic happens when you automate this—set up a separate account just for fun money and let it build quietly in the background. When something exciting pops up, you can say "yes" with confidence, knowing the money is already there.

But here's the hack: **Pre-plan your splurges.** Instead of impulsively spending every time an opportunity arises, create a list of experiences you want to prioritize. That way, when your bestie suggests a last-minute trip or tickets drop for your favorite artist, you're already prepared. This doesn't kill the spontaneity—it just ensures that your yes doesn't come with financial regret.

The Emotional Side of Spending on Fun

Let's be honest—there's an emotional weight to how we spend on fun. Sometimes, it's celebration spending. Other times, it's emotional escape. Either way, those transactions aren't just about the numbers. When you blow your budget on fun, it often carries a deeper story—one tied to how you see yourself and your place in your social world.

Take the social pressure, for instance. When your friends are out here living their best lives—booking lavish vacations, dining at the trendiest spots—it's easy to feel like you're missing out if you're not spending at the same pace. But here's the truth: You can opt in without overspending.

The trick is being honest with yourself about what's worth it. Are you spending on experiences that genuinely bring you joy—or are you paying to keep up? The difference is subtle but powerful. Real fun feels expansive and energizing. Performative spending, on the other hand, leaves you drained—emotionally and financially.

If you find yourself saying "yes" to plans that stretch your budget, try this: **Pause and ask yourself, "Is this a 'hell yes,' or am I doing this to avoid FOMO?"** Learning to trust your own definition of fun—not the one Instagram sells you—frees you from the guilt spiral of overextending yourself.

Recovering from Fun-Induced Financial Hangovers

We've all been there—the morning-after money anxiety. You wake up, scroll through your bank statement, and wonder if last night's fun was really worth the damage. The trick isn't to punish yourself—it's to build in recovery time.

First, **do a post-fun audit.** What did you spend, and how did it feel? If it was worth every penny, no regrets. If it wasn't, use that insight to adjust your future fun budget. The goal isn't to cut joy—it's to ensure your spending reflects what actually makes you happy.

Next, **balance the scales.** If a spontaneous splurge throws your cash flow off, course-correct without overcompensating. Maybe that means pausing non-essential spending for a week or redirecting future fun funds to cover the gap. The point is to take action without spiraling into guilt.

And finally, **treat fun spending as a learning curve.** Each time you overspend, you gather valuable data about what lights you up—and what doesn't. Over time, this helps you refine your fun budget so you're saying "yes" to the right things, not everything.

The best financial plans don't ignore joy—they prioritize it. Fun isn't a frivolous expense; it's an investment in your mental health, relationships, and overall happiness. And when you plan for it, you're not just protecting your bank account—you're giving yourself permission to enjoy life without the emotional and financial hangover.

So go ahead—have fun. Buy the concert tickets. Book the trip. Say yes to the things that make you feel alive. Just make sure your money is working with you, not against you. Because the real luxury isn't just having fun—it's being able to afford it without stress.

32

The Financial Audit (Without the Panic)

NOTHING SPIKES YOUR HEART RATE quite like confronting your bank account after a month (or three) of *vibes-first, budget-later* spending. Whether it's the mystery charges you forgot about or that one purchase you swore you needed but now feels... questionable, the idea of a financial audit can feel like you're willingly walking into an emotional battlefield. But here's the truth—avoiding your money doesn't make it any less real. What it *does* do is keep you trapped in a cycle where your bank account is constantly full of surprises—and not the fun kind.

A financial audit isn't about judgment or deprivation. It's a reality check—a way to face your finances head-on and actually *understand* where your money's going. It's the difference between feeling like your bank account is a black hole and feeling like you're in the driver's seat. And no, you don't need to be an Excel-loving finance bro to pull it off. All it takes is a little curiosity, some honest reflection, and a willingness to swap panic for empowerment.

Why Avoiding Your Finances Feels Easier (But Isn't)

Let's address the elephant in the room—why does the thought of auditing your money feel so *ugh*? For most of us, money isn't just about numbers—it's tied to feelings of security, self-worth, and even identity. If you grew up in a household where money was a constant stressor, those old anxieties might flare up every time you check your balance. Or maybe your spending habits have been your coping mechanism—retail therapy when life gets tough, spontaneous splurges when you're craving a win.

Ignoring your finances feels easier in the short term because it delays the discomfort. But here's the twist—what you avoid doesn't disappear. That sinking feeling when your card gets declined? That's your financial reality creeping back in. The power move is to face it head-on—not with judgment, but with curiosity. What's really going on under the surface? Where is your money quietly slipping away? And more importantly—how can you make it work *for* you instead of against you?

Forget the spreadsheets and complicated formulas for a second. At its core, a financial audit is just a fancy way of asking: *Where is my money going, and is it working for me?* Instead of treating it like a high-stakes exam, think of it as an investigation—a way to uncover clues about your financial habits without spiraling into panic.

Start by pulling the receipts—literally. Look at your last three months of bank and credit card statements. This gives you a wide enough window to spot patterns but isn't so overwhelming that you drown in data. You're not just looking at what you spend—you're asking yourself *why*.

Certain spending categories tend to be the biggest culprits for money drain. Dining out, impulse buys, and random subscriptions often slip under the radar. But don't judge yourself—get curious. Did those late-night Uber Eats orders happen because you were too busy to cook, or was it more of an emotional comfort thing? Are you paying for three streaming services when you only watch the same rom-com on repeat? Knowing the *why* behind your spending is where the magic happens—because once you see the patterns, you can actually change them.

Spotting the Sneaky Money Drains

Not all spending is obvious. Sure, you might know you spent a little too much on that "treat yourself" weekend, but the most dangerous money drains are the ones that quietly bleed your account dry.

Subscription creep is a prime suspect. That $10 here, $15 there adds up fast when you're not paying attention. Old gym memberships, apps you don't use, free trials that somehow became permanent residents—these stealth charges are easy to overlook. Doing a subscription audit is a game-changer. Cancel what you don't actively use, and be ruthless. If it doesn't spark joy or deliver value, it's not worth the monthly charge.

Then, there are the "invisible luxuries"—small indulgences that feel harmless but pile up. Think daily coffee runs, delivery fees, and those "just a little something" shopping trips. On their own, they seem innocent, but over time? They quietly siphon your financial power. This doesn't mean cutting out every joy in life—it means making intentional choices instead of autopiloting through spending.

The Power of Regular Financial Check-Ins

One audit won't solve everything. The key is turning financial awareness into a regular habit. Think of it like a skincare routine—checking in consistently is how you catch small issues before they become full-blown breakouts.

Monthly check-ins give you a pulse on your money flow without the overwhelm. Pick a day—maybe it's the first Sunday of the month—and make it a ritual. Light a candle, pour yourself a fancy drink, and review your spending with curiosity, not criticism. Where did your money go? Did your spending align with what actually matters to you? And most importantly—how do you feel about it?

If something feels off, that's a signal—not a failure. Maybe you realized you're overspending on convenience because you're overworked. That's not just a financial issue—it's a life issue. Use your check-ins to adjust not just your spending, but how you're caring for yourself.

Mapping Your Money (Without the Overwhelm)

A "money map" is basically a blueprint for your financial future. It's not just about what you're spending—it's about where you're *going*. Without a clear map, your money tends to wander, and so do your goals.

Start simple:

Short-Term Wins: What do you want to achieve in the next 3-6 months? Maybe it's padding your emergency fund, paying off a small debt, or saving for a treat-yourself moment.

Mid-Term Moves: Where do you want to be financially in the next 1-3 years? This could mean upgrading your living situation, building a vacation fund, or tackling bigger debts.

Long-Term Glow-Up: What does future-you want? Retirement may sound far away, but starting now means your money works harder over time. Think of this as the foundation for your "rich person era."

By mapping out your goals, you give your money a job. And when every dollar has a purpose, you're less likely to waste it on things that don't serve you.

A financial audit isn't about punishment—it's about power. It's the difference between feeling like your money is something that happens *to* you and knowing it's something you can shape and control. The first time you do it, it might feel messy. That's normal. But each time you check in, you're reclaiming ownership—making your finances work for your life, not the other way around.

So take a breath. Open your bank app. And remember—your money isn't the enemy. It's a tool. And you? You're the one holding the reins.

33

The 50/30/20 Rule (But Make It Personal)

BUDGETING ADVICE OFTEN FEELS LIKE a one-size-fits-all sweater—technically functional, but not exactly tailored to your life. Enter the 50/30/20 rule, the budgeting framework that promises a simple breakdown: 50% for needs, 30% for wants, and 20% for savings and debt repayment. It sounds easy enough—until life happens. Because honestly, what counts as a "need" versus a "want" when your mental health relies on your weekly pilates class? And how are you supposed to save 20% when your paycheck barely makes it to the end of the month?

Here's the truth: the 50/30/20 rule works as a starting point, not a rigid commandment. Your lifestyle, your goals, and your financial reality are uniquely yours—so your budget should reflect that. Making this classic rule personal is about building a framework that feels supportive, not suffocating. Let's ditch the cookie-cutter version and find a balance that fits your life right now while still leaving room to grow.

Where Did the 50/30/20 Rule Come From Anyway?

The 50/30/20 rule isn't some random internet hack—it actually has political roots. It was popularized by Senator Elizabeth Warren and her daughter Amelia Warren Tyagi in their book *All Your Worth: The Ultimate Lifetime Money Plan*. Their goal? To create a budgeting method that was simple enough to follow without requiring you to analyze every penny.

The breakdown looks like this:

- **50% for Needs:** The non-negotiables—rent or mortgage, utilities, groceries, transportation, insurance, and other basic living expenses.
- **30% for Wants:** The fun stuff—dining out, streaming subscriptions, travel, hobbies, and the things that make life enjoyable.
- **20% for Savings and Debt:** Building your future—this includes emergency funds, retirement savings, paying off debt, and other long-term financial goals.

Sounds reasonable, right? But here's the catch—life isn't divided into perfect thirds. Depending on where you live, what you earn, and how you define your priorities, those categories might need some serious tweaking. That's where personalization comes in.

Why the 50/30/20 Rule Feels Out of Touch for Many

Let's be honest—50% for needs can feel laughably unrealistic when you're living in a city where rent takes a massive bite out of your paycheck. And for those juggling student loans, medical bills, or supporting family members, that tidy 20% for savings can feel more like wishful thinking. Meanwhile, the 30% for "wants" sounds nice—until you realize how much of your joy comes from those little indulgences that technically aren't essential but feel deeply necessary.

This isn't about blaming yourself for not fitting into a rigid mold—it's about understanding that a framework is only useful if it adapts to your reality. If your needs take up 60% of your income, that doesn't mean you're failing—it just means your life isn't a neat pie chart. The key is figuring out how to adjust the formula while still prioritizing what matters to you.

Here's how you can customize the rule to fit you:

Step 1: Start with Your Actual Numbers

Before you can personalize anything, you need to know where your money is actually going. Pull up your last three months of bank and credit card statements and track your spending across the three categories—needs, wants, and savings/debt. No judgment, just facts. What percentage of your income is going to each?

You might find that your "needs" category is higher than 50%, especially if you're in a high-cost-of-living area or dealing with medical or family obligations. That's okay. The goal isn't to force your life to fit the rule—it's to make the rule fit your life.

Step 2: Define What Really Counts as a "Need"

One person's luxury is another person's sanity-saver. Is therapy a need or a want? What about your morning latte that keeps you from losing your mind? While traditional budgeting rules treat needs as basic survival, your reality is more nuanced. Think about what keeps your life functional—not just physically, but emotionally.

Step 3: Adjust the Percentages to Match Your Reality

If your "needs" take up 60% of your income, you could shrink your "wants" to 20% and lower savings to 10% temporarily. Or, if your lifestyle is low-maintenance, maybe your "wants" stay closer to 20% while you aggressively save 30%. The magic is in the flexibility.

Consider your current season of life. Are you saving up for a big goal? Prioritize the savings bucket. Hustling through a demanding work period? Allow for a bigger "wants" category to support your well-being. This is your budget—there are no universal rules.

When Life Changes, So Should Your Budget

Your budget isn't meant to be static. As your income shifts, your lifestyle evolves, and your goals change, your financial plan should flex with you. A newly-minted graduate working their first job will have a different budget balance than someone established in their career, just as someone starting a family will prioritize differently than someone living solo.

When you get a raise, it's tempting to increase your "wants" spending—but consider directing at least part of that extra cash toward savings or paying off debt. Similarly, if you hit a rough patch financially, adjusting down your savings temporarily while maintaining essentials can keep you afloat without guilt.

The trick? Regular check-ins. Schedule a monthly "money date" with yourself—grab your favorite drink, pull out your spending tracker, and see if your current budget still fits your life. When something feels off, adjust. No shame, no stress—just a constant evolution toward a budget that works *for* you, not against you.

Maybe your ratio looks more like 60/25/15 or even 70/20/10. That's not a failure—it's a reflection of your life right now. What matters most is that your spending aligns with what you value and that you're consistently working toward your goals, even if the pace is slower than some Instagram finance guru suggests.

Personalizing your budget is about making space for your priorities without drowning in rigid expectations. Some months you'll save less. Other months you'll treat yourself a little more. The balance is yours to define—and that's where the real financial freedom lies.

At the end of the day, the 50/30/20 rule is a tool—not a cage. Let it guide you, but don't let it box you in. Your money, your rules, your glow-up—on your terms.

PART 8

Digital Spending Detox

34

The Algorithm Wants You Broke

MAYBE YOU'RE CATCHING UP ON your favorite creator's latest post or just killing time between meetings. But before you know it, there's a perfectly targeted ad flashing on your screen—those sneakers you didn't know you needed or a "life-changing" gadget promising to streamline your mornings. One click, a couple of taps, and bam—you've just spent money you didn't plan to. Welcome to the world of algorithm-driven spending, where the lines between browsing and buying are blurrier than ever.

If it feels like your paycheck evaporates the moment you touch your phone, that's not an accident. Big Tech has perfected the art of making you spend, and those algorithms? They're not playing fair. Every ad you see, every "limited-time offer" that pops up, and even the content in your feed is engineered to trigger your impulse-buying instincts. The result? Your money is quietly slipping into the digital void while your cart overflows with things you probably didn't need in the first place.

Understanding how these algorithms work—and how to outsmart them—is your secret weapon for staying in control. Because here's the truth: You don't need to quit your favorite apps to protect your bank account. You just need to stop letting the algorithm call the shots.

Algorithms aren't just lines of code—they're finely tuned

psychological machines designed to know you better than you know yourself. Every like, search, and scroll is data. That pair of jeans you casually checked out last week? The algorithm remembers. The candle haul your bestie posted on Instagram? It knows you probably want those, too.

And it's not just what you actively engage with—the algorithm is watching everything. How long you pause on a post, the hashtags you follow, even the types of content your friends interact with—it all feeds into a system that curates your digital world. And here's the kicker: these systems are designed to keep you spending, not saving.

Impulse spending has never been easier. "Buy Now, Pay Later" options make purchases feel painless, while same-day delivery eliminates the wait time that might've given you second thoughts. Even those harmless-seeming "suggested for you" product carousels are a well-crafted trap, nudging you toward purchases under the illusion of personal choice. The more you engage, the smarter the algorithm gets—training itself to deliver temptations you find impossible to resist.

When Social Media Becomes a Spending Minefield

Social media isn't just where you go to catch up with friends anymore—it's a 24/7 shopping mall disguised as entertainment. Platforms like Instagram, TikTok, and Pinterest seamlessly blur the line between content and commerce, turning everyday scrolling into a full-blown shopping spree.

"TikTok made me buy it" isn't just a cute trend—it's a multi-billion-dollar spending culture. Whether it's a viral beauty product or a kitchen gadget promising to revolutionize your mornings, these posts hit differently because they feel personal. You're not just seeing a faceless ad—you're watching a real person rave about how this one thing changed their life. And when the "shop now" button is right there? Game over.

Influencer marketing only amplifies this effect. When someone you admire posts about their latest fashion find or skincare obsession, it doesn't feel like a sales pitch—it feels like a friend sharing a secret. The trust factor is real, and brands know it. They're betting on the fact that you're more likely to buy from someone you feel connected to, and the algorithm makes sure those products show up at just the right moment—usually when you're most vulnerable to spending.

Outsmart the algorithm.

Beating the algorithm at its own game starts with awareness. Once you see the strings being pulled, you're no longer a puppet to digital spending traps. But awareness alone won't cut it—you need practical strategies to break free.

1. **Unfollow the Temptation**: Let's be real—if your feed is flooded with influencers pushing "must-haves," your wallet is in constant danger. Take a hard look at the accounts you follow. Are they inspiring you, or are they triggering you to spend? Curate your feed intentionally. Unfollow (or mute) accounts that fuel impulse buying and replace them with content that supports your financial goals.
2. **Disrupt the Data Trail**: Algorithms work by collecting data, so cutting off their fuel supply weakens their grip. Regularly clear your browsing history and cookies, especially after window shopping. Use privacy-focused search engines or enable "do not track" settings to limit how much data is collected about you.
    Browser extensions like *AdBlock* and *uBlock Origin* can also reduce the number of targeted ads you see, while apps like *Freedom* or *StayFocusd* help curb endless scrolling sessions

that lead to impulse spending.
3. **Pause Before You Purchase**
Impulse buys thrive on urgency—limited-time offers and flash sales prey on your fear of missing out (FOMO). Combat this by implementing a "pause" rule. Before making any unplanned purchase, wait at least 24 hours. This cooling-off period helps you separate fleeting desires from genuine needs. If you're feeling extra bold, try the 30-day list method: whenever you want to buy something non-essential, write it down along with the date. If you still want it after 30 days, it's probably worth it. If not? Consider it money saved.
4. **Make the Algorithm Work for You**
You can actually "train" your algorithm to prioritize content that aligns with your goals. Engage more with financial education posts, saving hacks, and mindful living accounts. The more you interact with these topics, the more the algorithm will serve you content that empowers, rather than drains, your bank account.

Staying Mindful in a Swipe-to-Buy World

At the end of the day, the algorithm isn't going anywhere—but your financial sanity doesn't have to suffer. Practicing digital mindfulness means recognizing when you're being nudged toward spending and choosing to pause instead of react.

Consider adopting regular "digital detox" days where you unplug from social media entirely. Not only does this give your brain a break from the constant consumption cycle, but it also makes you more conscious of how much influence these platforms have over your daily decisions.

And when you do spend? Do it on your terms. There's nothing wrong with treating yourself—but the real flex is knowing that you're in control, not some faceless algorithm pulling the strings. Your wallet deserves better than to be at the mercy of tech giants.

35

The 3-Click Rule

PICTURE THIS: YOU'RE CASUALLY SCROLLING through your favorite online store. There it is—a sleek pair of boots that promises to elevate your entire vibe. Before you even register what's happening, you've clicked "Add to Cart." A few taps later, the confirmation email pings. Another impulse buy, locked and loaded. And sure, the rush of a new purchase feels good—for a moment. But when that credit card statement rolls in, the excitement fades fast.

Impulse spending online isn't just easy—it's designed to be. Retailers know that the quicker and smoother the buying process, the more likely you are to part with your cash. And in a world where one-click checkouts and "Buy Now, Pay Later" options reign supreme, your money is more vulnerable than ever. Enter the 3-Click Rule: a simple, brilliant strategy to slow down the spending spiral and reclaim control before your cart takes over.

This isn't about deleting your favorite shopping apps or swearing off online stores forever. It's about adding intentional friction—tiny roadblocks that disrupt the autopilot spending mode and force you to think before you buy. By making the process just a little harder, you give yourself the breathing room to decide whether a purchase is a genuine want or just a fleeting craving.

Why Online Shopping Feels So Addictive

There's a reason it feels almost too easy to blow your budget online—it's by design. Every aspect of an e-commerce site is crafted to make spending effortless. From the moment you land on a webpage, subtle psychological tricks work behind the scenes to push you closer to that "Confirm Purchase" button.

One of the biggest culprits? Instant gratification. In the pre-digital age, buying something required effort—physically going to a store, waiting in line, and handing over cash. That delay gave your brain time to process the purchase and weigh whether it was worth it. Now? The lag time between "I want it" and "I own it" has basically vanished.

Retailers exploit this through what psychologists call "frictionless spending." Fewer steps between wanting and buying means fewer chances for you to second-guess the purchase. Features like saved payment information, one-click checkout, and digital wallets are engineered to eliminate those precious moments where you might pause and reconsider. Add to that the emotional pull of flash sales and limited-time offers, and suddenly, resisting a spontaneous purchase feels nearly impossible.

But here's the kicker—slowing down even slightly can dramatically reduce impulse buys. That's where the 3-Click Rule shines.

What Is the 3-Click Rule?

The 3-Click Rule is simple: never buy anything online unless it takes at least three deliberate steps to complete the purchase. The goal is to add friction—those tiny roadblocks that interrupt the automatic spending reflex and give you a mental "cool-off" window.

When you force yourself to slow down, you engage your rational brain (the part that handles long-term planning) instead of letting your impulsive brain run wild. It's not about making spending impossible—it's about making it intentional.

Here's how to put it into action:

Step 1: Disable One-Click Checkout

Convenience is the enemy of mindful spending. If your payment details are automatically stored on every shopping platform, it's time to break up with that habit. Delete saved cards from your go-to sites and disable any express checkout options. When you have to manually enter payment details, you buy yourself valuable thinking time—and that pause is often enough to derail an unnecessary purchase.

Step 2: Add a Deliberate Barrier

Introduce a small but intentional obstacle between you and the "Buy Now" button. This could mean requiring yourself to search for a discount code, opening a new browser tab to read reviews, or even logging out of your account after each purchase. These extra steps create a speed bump that disrupts impulse decision-making.

One clever hack? Switch to incognito mode when browsing shopping sites. This blocks auto-fill information, so every purchase requires you to manually enter your details—slowing you down while making you think twice.

Step 3: Implement a 24-Hour Rule

Before finalizing any non-essential purchase, let it sit in your cart for a full day. That cooling-off period works wonders. More often than not, what feels urgent in the heat of the moment loses its appeal after a bit of time. If you still want the item 24 hours later, fine. But if the urge fades? Consider it a win for your wallet.

Why Making Things Harder Works

It sounds counterintuitive—aren't we all about making life easier? But when it comes to your spending habits, a little difficulty is a game-changer. Psychologists call this "decision friction," and it's one of the most effective ways to curb impulsivity.

When spending is too easy, your brain doesn't have time to engage in thoughtful decision-making. By adding intentional barriers, you interrupt the emotional rush that drives most impulse buys. This pause activates your prefrontal cortex—the part of your brain responsible for logic, planning, and long-term thinking. In other words, it gives you space to ask: *Do I actually want this, or am I just falling for the moment?*

Plus, making the purchase process slightly more annoying forces you to prioritize what really matters. When every transaction takes a little more effort, you're less likely to waste energy (and cash) on things you don't truly value.

Digital Hacks to Reinforce the 3-Click Rule

If you're serious about slowing down your online spending, technology can actually work *for* you, not against you. Here are a few easy digital hacks to keep impulse buys in check:

Install a Browser Extension – Tools like *Impulse Blocker* and *Icebox* delay or block shopping sites, requiring you to confirm purchases after a set waiting period.

Use a Prepaid Card – For non-essential spending, load a fixed amount of cash onto a prepaid card. This gives you a hard limit and prevents overspending.

Enable Purchase Limits – Many banking apps let you set spending limits on specific categories or stores. Use this to enforce financial boundaries.

Unsubscribe from Temptation – If you're bombarded with promo emails, unsubscribe aggressively. Less exposure equals fewer impulse buys.

The 3-Click Rule isn't about depriving yourself—it's about making intentional choices. Not every purchase needs to go through a rigorous waiting period. Essentials? Skip the friction. But for everything else—especially luxury buys or "treat yourself" moments—stick to the rule like your bank balance depends on it (because it does).

The bottom line? You're not at the mercy of every flashy ad or sneaky algorithm. With a few smart tweaks, you can enjoy online shopping *without* draining your wallet. And trust—there's nothing more powerful than spending on your own terms.

36

Unsubscribing from Broke Culture

BROKE CULTURE ISN'T JUST A meme; it's a whole vibe—a dangerously relatable one. It's the playful "I'm broke, but let's go out anyway" energy. The *"treat yourself"* mentality that somehow justifies a $7 latte every morning. The constant swirl of sales, influencer hauls, and "buy now, worry later" messaging that makes you feel like spending is not just normal—it's inevitable. And here's the thing: it's not an accident.

Brands are *really* good at making you feel like your wallet should always be open. From those hyper-targeted Instagram ads to limited-time offers that seem *too* good to miss, every digital corner you scroll through is designed to keep you spending. But what if you could rewrite the narrative? What if your money could work *for* you instead of flowing out faster than it comes in? That starts with unsubscribing—not just from endless promotional emails but from the mindset that tells you it's normal to stay broke while keeping up appearances.

It's not your imagination—spending feels easier than ever, and that's by design. We live in an age where convenience reigns supreme. Algorithms know your weak spots better than you do. Your social media feeds? They're carefully curated storefronts, showing you exactly what you never knew you needed. And the emotional pull is real.

At its core, broke culture feeds on three things:

1. **FOMO (Fear of Missing Out):** That internal panic when you see everyone living their best lives—jetting off on vacations, wearing the latest drops, dining at trendy spots—and you feel like you're falling behind if you don't join in.
2. **Instant Gratification:** Why wait when you can have it now? With one-click purchases and Buy Now, Pay Later schemes, there's no need to delay a single desire.
3. **Social Validation:** A new purchase isn't just about the item—it's about sharing it. Posting your latest splurge on Instagram is part of the experience, and likes feel like mini rewards for your spending.

But here's the twist: while broke culture feels fun and effortless in the moment, it's a fast-track to financial stress. And breaking free from that cycle requires more than just cutting up your credit card—it's about consciously rewiring the way you interact with money and media.

The Psychology of "Spend More, Stay Broke"

Ever wondered why you're more likely to buy something when it's "limited edition" or on a countdown timer? That's called **scarcity marketing**, and it works by triggering your brain's loss aversion. The fear of missing out overrides rational thinking, making you click "buy" before you even process whether you actually *want* the thing.

And brands? They know exactly how to play the game. Whether it's personalized ads that follow you across platforms or influencers who make every product feel like a must-have, the line between marketing and reality is blurrier than ever. Each post, ad, and email is designed to make you feel like spending is the only way to keep up—and they're *really* good at it.

The good news? You don't have to be a passive participant in this cycle. You can take back control by unsubscribing—literally and metaphorically—from the messages that keep you stuck in broke culture.

Step One: Clean Up Your Digital Space

Your inbox and social feeds are like prime real estate for broke culture, and if you're serious about cutting back, it's time to declutter.

1. **Unsubscribe Aggressively:** Go through your email and unsubscribe from every store, brand, or platform that constantly pushes discounts and "exclusive offers." If you don't see the sale, you won't be tempted by it.
2. **Unfollow (or Mute) Spending Triggers:** That influencer who's always flaunting the latest luxury buys? The brands that keep teasing you with new arrivals? Hit unfollow or mute their content. You're not missing out—you're protecting your peace (and your bank account).
3. **Use Digital Boundaries:** Tools like *Unroll.Me* can mass unsubscribe you from marketing emails, while browser extensions like *AdBlock* or *Impulse Blocker* can hide tempting ads altogether.

Step Two: Rewire Your Relationship with "Want"

Here's a hard truth: most of what we want isn't rooted in actual need—it's about emotion. And brands are experts at exploiting those emotions. When you see a product that makes your heart race, ask yourself these questions:

Is this solving a real problem, or am I just chasing a feeling? Would I still want this if no one else could see it? Am I buying this for "future me," or is it just a quick fix for today's boredom?

By pausing to interrogate your desires, you'll start recognizing just how often your spending is emotionally charged—not logical.

Step Three: Curate a Feed That Supports Your Financial Goals

If your social media feeds are full of spending triggers, flip the script. You control the algorithm more than you realize, and with a little intention, you can curate content that inspires better money habits rather than draining your wallet.

Seek out accounts that empower smart spending and saving. From minimalist living advocates to financial educators, there are influencers out there who will *help* you grow wealth rather than waste it.

Algorithms respond to your behavior. If you want to see less shopping content, stop liking, sharing, or clicking on it. Instead, engage with content about saving hacks, financial literacy, and intentional living.

Pin or save posts that reflect your bigger financial goals—whether it's traveling debt-free, building an emergency fund, or achieving early retirement. Use this as a visual reminder of why you're unsubscribing from broke culture in the first place.

Step Four: Normalize Saying "No"

Broke culture thrives on peer pressure—whether it's social events, group trips, or friends who are always down to "just split it." And while it's tempting to go along, setting financial boundaries isn't just healthy—it's essential.

You don't have to opt out of fun entirely, but you *can* be selective. Practice phrases like:

"I'm saving for something bigger, so I'll pass this time."

"I'm down for a hangout—let's make it budget-friendly."

"I'd love to join, but I'm keeping an eye on my spending this month."

The people who care about you will respect your boundaries. And those who don't? Well, that's a whole other conversation.

Unsubscribing from broke culture isn't just about spending less—it's about living more intentionally. When you stop letting brands, algorithms, and social pressure dictate your financial decisions, you reclaim the power to design a life aligned with what truly matters to you.

And here's the real flex: there's nothing cooler than having your finances under control while still living your best life. So, click "unsubscribe," hit "unfollow," and watch your bank account (and your peace of mind) grow.

PART 9

Money & Relationships

37

Love, But Make It Budget-Friendly

LOVE MIGHT BE PRICELESS, BUT dinner dates, vacations, and anniversaries? Not so much. In a world where grand gestures are glamorized, it's easy to feel like your relationship needs a hefty price tag to thrive. But the truth is, romance doesn't have to come with a financial hangover. What really matters is how you and your partner communicate, compromise, and find joy—whether it's a candlelit dinner or a Netflix binge in sweatpants. And when it comes to money? The sooner you tackle those "awkward" conversations, the stronger your foundation will be.

At the core of every relationship is an invisible financial thread. Who pays for what? How do you handle differences in spending habits? What happens when one of you is a saver and the other's a "live in the moment" spender? The goal isn't to agree on everything—it's to create a shared money mindset that respects both your needs and your budget. So, whether you're dating casually or deep in your *forever* era, it's time to make love budget-friendly—without killing the vibe.

Money and love are two of the most emotionally charged topics in life, and when you mix them? Things get messy—fast. Society is full of outdated money tropes: the idea that one person should foot the bill, that talking about money is *taboo*, or that "if you love me, you won't care what I spend." But here's the reality: financial compatibility is a major player in long-term relationship happiness.

It's not just about how much you make—it's about how you view, spend, and save it. Are you the type to splurge on experiences while your partner hoards every penny for the future? Do you believe "what's mine is yours," or are you more of a "separate accounts forever" person? These differences don't have to be deal-breakers—but ignoring them is a recipe for resentment.

Money talks aren't unromantic. They're a sign you're building something real. The trick? Start early, stay open, and approach it like a team. After all, you're not fighting each other—you're fighting the problem.

The Awkward Art of Splitting Costs

Whether you're splitting appetizers or planning a vacation, money can get weird fast. Who pays on dates? Should costs be split 50/50, or is it fairer to go by income? There's no universal rule, but the key is to find a rhythm that feels fair—and to keep the conversation honest.

If one partner earns significantly more, a strict 50/50 split might feel lopsided. Instead, try a **proportional approach**—where you contribute based on what you earn. If you're living together, you might decide that one covers rent while the other handles utilities and groceries. The goal isn't perfect equality—it's equity.

And for those first few dates? There's nothing wrong with the classic "I got this, you get the next one" flow. Generosity shouldn't be gendered, and keeping score isn't sexy. If you're both showing up and contributing in a way that fits your means, you're doing it right.

Money Talks Without the Ick

Bringing up money can feel like you're pulling out a spreadsheet on date night—but it doesn't have to be stiff or transactional. The key is timing and tone. Don't wait until you're knee-deep in an argument to discuss how to split bills. Instead, treat these talks as a way to strengthen your partnership.

Here's how to ease into the conversation:

Start Light: Share your earliest money memory or how your family handled finances. This opens the door to deeper talks without diving straight into "So, what's your credit score?"

Dream Together: Instead of focusing on spreadsheets, talk about what you want your future to look like—travel, buying a home, or financial freedom. Then, work backward to see how your spending aligns.

Frame It as a Team Effort: Instead of "You spend too much," try "How can we create a system that works for both of us?" It's about finding solutions—not assigning blame.

Money convos aren't a one-and-done thing. Relationships evolve, and so do financial needs. Regular check-ins—whether it's over coffee or during a cozy night in—keep you aligned and prevent little money tensions from turning into major blowouts.

Date Nights That Don't Break the Bank

Contrary to what Instagram suggests, love isn't measured in Michelin stars and surprise getaways. Some of the best memories come from the simplest moments—and your relationship doesn't need a luxury budget to thrive.

Low-cost doesn't mean low-effort. With a little creativity, you can keep the spark alive without setting your bank account on fire:

DIY Date Nights: Cook a fancy dinner together, complete

with candles and a playlist. It's cheaper (and often more fun) than a restaurant.

Outdoor Adventures: Pack a picnic, go stargazing, or take a sunset walk. Romance is free—nature delivers.

At-Home Movie Marathon: Recreate a theater vibe with popcorn, cozy blankets, and a lineup of your favorite films.

Free Local Events: Keep an eye on community happenings—art fairs, outdoor concerts, or free museum days are easy wins.

It's not about how much you spend—it's about how intentional you are with your time. The real flex? Showing love in ways that are thoughtful, not just expensive.

When Financial Goals Don't Match

So, what happens when one of you is saving for the future while the other's living like there's no tomorrow? Financial mismatches are common—but they don't have to be a dealbreaker.

Step one? Understand *why* your partner approaches money the way they do. People's financial habits are often shaped by childhood experiences and personal fears. Maybe they grew up with scarcity, or perhaps they view money as a source of freedom. Either way, there's usually a deeper reason behind their spending or saving style.

The solution isn't to change each other—it's to find middle ground. If you're a saver dating a spender, consider setting separate "fun money" budgets so you both feel free without guilt. If one of you is laser-focused on long-term goals, balance it by leaving room for spontaneous pleasures.

And when in doubt? Return to the shared vision. If you're working toward a common future—whether it's buying a home, traveling the world, or simply staying debt-free—those big-picture goals will guide you toward compromises that feel right.

Love + Money = Power Couple Energy

Money isn't the most romantic topic—but getting on the same page financially is one of the best things you can do for your relationship. When you and your partner work together toward shared goals, you're not just securing your financial future—you're strengthening your bond.

And here's the best part: the most meaningful moments in a relationship rarely come with a price tag. Love doesn't live in receipts or grand gestures—it's in the small, intentional ways you show up for each other, every day. So, ditch the broke-culture pressure, set your own rules, and keep building a life where both your hearts—and your wallets—are full.

38

Financial Boundaries in Family Drama

MONEY AND FAMILY—A COMBINATION AS tricky as group chats with too many opinions. When love and finances collide, things can get messy fast. Whether it's a sibling asking for a "small" loan, parents subtly hinting for help, or relatives assuming you're the family ATM, it's hard to balance generosity with self-preservation. The emotional weight of family dynamics can make saying "no" feel like a betrayal, but here's the truth: protecting your financial future isn't selfish—it's smart.

The tricky part? Money issues in families rarely exist in a vacuum. There's always a backstory—a mix of cultural expectations, childhood patterns, and unspoken power dynamics. Maybe you grew up watching your parents struggle, and now there's pressure to "pay it forward." Or perhaps you're the "successful" one, and everyone assumes you're doing fine, even when you're quietly drowning in bills. The expectations are rarely spelled out, but the guilt? Oh, it's loud.

Boundaries aren't about shutting people out—they're about keeping your peace intact. And when it comes to family and money, drawing those lines is essential if you want to help without losing yourself (or your savings) in the process.

Here's the thing about family: history makes everything feel personal. Unlike a friend borrowing twenty bucks, family financial requests are layered with emotional ties, past favors, and the ever-present "you owe us" energy. The unspoken script? If you love us, you'll help. And if you don't? Cue the guilt trip.

This pressure can hit especially hard if you're seen as "the responsible one." Maybe you're the first in the family to achieve financial stability—or maybe your ability to say "I can't" feels complicated because you once relied on their support. Either way, the emotional math doesn't always add up. You love your family, but love alone won't cover your rent.

And let's not forget the "invisible tax" many people pay within their families—unspoken expectations to fund holidays, emergencies, or "just this once" requests that seem to multiply. Whether it's cultural norms or birth-order dynamics, some people are quietly carrying the weight for everyone else.

Let's be honest—saying "no" to family feels… heavy. You worry about being seen as cold or ungrateful. But constantly saying "yes" when you can't afford to (or simply don't want to) leads to resentment—and drained bank accounts. The goal is to find a middle ground where you protect your finances while still showing love.

Here's how to turn down family financial requests with grace (and without the awkward fallout):

Be Clear, Not Cruel: You don't need a 10-slide PowerPoint explaining your budget. A simple, firm response works: "I'm not in a position to help right now." You're not required to give a TED Talk on your financial limits—no is a full sentence.

Blame the Budget: Shift the focus off your personal feelings and onto a neutral third party—your financial plan. Try, "I've set some strict savings goals and can't afford to help at the moment."

It feels less personal while still being firm.

Offer Non-Financial Support: Just because you can't give money doesn't mean you can't help. Offer your time, resources, or skills instead. "I can't loan money, but I'd be happy to help you job hunt or brainstorm other solutions."

Stick to Your No: Some family members are masters of the second ask—the "oh, but it's *just this once*" plea. Don't cave. Your first no should be your final answer, no matter how much they push.

Saying no won't always feel good—but neither does sacrificing your financial stability for someone else's expectations.

Even when you know you're doing the right thing, the guilt can sneak up on you. It's that little voice whispering, *"But they need you..."* Here's how to quiet the guilt without abandoning your boundaries:

1. Separate Love from Obligation: Saying no to money doesn't mean saying no to love. You can care deeply for your family without becoming their financial safety net.
2. Check Your Inner Script: If you grew up believing you're responsible for everyone's well-being, it's time to rewrite that narrative. Your worth isn't measured by how much you give.
3. Know Your Limits: It's okay to prioritize your financial goals. You can't pour from an empty cup—or in this case, an overdrawn account.
4. Celebrate the Long Game: By protecting your finances now, you're setting yourself up to be more generous down the road—on *your* terms.

The guilt won't vanish overnight, but reminding yourself why these boundaries matter will help you stay firm.

The Family Tax: When Helping Hurts

The family tax is real—and it doesn't just come in cash form. It's the emotional toll of being the "go-to" person. It's the tension that creeps in when you feel more like a bank than a loved one.

If you've fallen into the family ATM trap, there's are ways to recalibrate.

Decide in advance how much you're willing (and able) to give without resentment. Whether it's a yearly cap or a case-by-case basis, defining your limit protects both your wallet and your emotional health.

Treat financial help like a business decision. Are you willing to gift, but not loan? Will you only help in emergencies? Clarifying your policy makes future asks easier to navigate.

If a family member's financial habits are consistently chaotic, loans won't fix the problem—education and support will. Offer resources or guidance instead of becoming their backup plan.

Let's be real—setting financial boundaries won't always go over smoothly. Some family members may take it personally. Others might gossip or try to guilt-trip you back into their wallet. Here's how to hold the line:

Stand Firm with Compassion: Be kind, but unwavering. "I love you, but I can't help financially. I hope you understand." Repeat as needed.

Expect Pushback: It's normal for people to test new boundaries. Their discomfort doesn't mean you're doing something wrong.

Protect Your Peace: If certain family dynamics are draining, limit your exposure. You can love people without giving them constant access to your emotional and financial energy.

At the heart of it, setting financial boundaries with family isn't about being stingy—it's about self-respect. It's a way of saying, *I love you, but I also love myself enough to protect my future.*

When you stop overextending yourself, you create space for healthier, more balanced relationships—ones where love isn't measured by dollar signs. And in the long run? That's the kind of family bond that money could never buy.

39

Friendships & Finances: The Real Talk

MONEY AND FRIENDSHIP—TWO THINGS THAT feel like they should never mix, yet somehow, they always do. Whether it's splitting bills, planning trips, or navigating financial differences, money has a sneaky way of showing up in your closest relationships. And if you've ever felt that awkward tension when a friend suggests a plan your bank account doesn't vibe with, you're not alone. In a world where brunches are bottomless and "let's split it evenly" can send you spiraling, it's no wonder that money can make or break even the strongest bonds. The truth is, avoiding money conversations with friends doesn't make the tension go away—it just buries it under layers of unspoken expectations and quiet resentment. And while no one wants to be "that friend" who brings up budgets at every turn, there's a sweet spot between being honest and being that one person who makes everything weird. So, how do you keep your financial peace without turning every hangout into a budget committee meeting? It starts with understanding one simple truth: your financial comfort zone matters, and real friendships can handle those conversations.

Let's talk about the unspoken rules first. Social norms often push the idea that true friendship means never talking about money—like it's too crass or uncomfortable. But in reality, avoiding the money talk can lead to misunderstandings and even fractured relationships. Picture this: a group vacation gets planned, and no one talks about cost expectations upfront. Suddenly, you're knee-deep in hotel bills you didn't approve of, awkwardly watching the group Venmo requests roll in. It's easy to feel trapped in these moments—caught between wanting to maintain friendships and not wanting to empty your savings to do it.

The fix? Be upfront before the costs spiral. If a trip's being planned, talk openly about your financial comfort level early on. It's not about being cheap—it's about being clear. You don't need to justify your financial decisions with an emotional monologue. A simple "I'm keeping an eye on my spending right now—can we aim for a more budget-friendly option?" works just fine. Friends who respect you won't need a TED Talk to understand that you're managing your money wisely.

And when it comes to those spontaneous group outings, things can get even trickier. We've all been there—sitting at the table, stomach sinking as someone orders a second round of cocktails you weren't planning to pay for. The "let's split the bill evenly" routine may be convenient, but it's not always fair. If you're someone who sticks to your budget while others go wild, footing an equal share can feel frustrating. Speaking up in these moments doesn't make you stingy—it makes you honest. The key is to communicate in a way that's casual but clear. You can say, "Hey, I only had the pasta—mind if I just cover my share?" Nine times out of ten, people will understand. And if they don't? That's a friendship flag worth noticing.

Loaning money is another landmine entirely. It's easy to

assume that lending a friend cash is harmless—it's what good friends do, right? But the reality is, mixing finances with friendships can blur boundaries fast. Before you open your wallet, ask yourself a simple question: "If I never get this money back, will it damage our friendship?" If the answer isn't a clear no, pause. It's better to give money as a gift if you can afford to—no strings, no expectations—than to create an emotional IOU that hovers over your friendship. And if you're on the other side of the equation—needing to borrow—be honest, upfront, and realistic about your ability to repay.

The toughest situations come when friendships hit financial mismatches. Maybe you're grinding to pay off debt while your friends are living that 'treat yourself' lifestyle. It can feel alienating when their version of "casual plans" means a $200 night out, while yours involves Netflix and home-cooked pasta. But the best friendships thrive on honesty. It's okay to say, "I'm watching my spending, but I'd love to hang out—let's do something low-key." If your friends care more about your company than the price tag, they'll happily adjust.

Friendship and finances will always be intertwined, whether you talk about it or not. But owning your money boundaries doesn't make you a bad friend—it makes you a smart one. And the friendships that stick around? Those are the ones where honesty, not spending, is the real currency.

40

Your Financial Era (And How to Own It)

THERE'S A MOMENT WHEN YOUR relationship with money shifts—from surviving to thriving. It's not about hitting a specific number in your bank account or finally buying the "dream" handbag. It's about stepping into a mindset where you control your finances, not the other way around. This is your financial era—where you own your choices, spend with intention, and build a life that reflects both your values and your vibe. And the best part? You get to define exactly what that looks like.

Owning your financial era isn't about chasing perfection or following rigid rules—it's about crafting a money style that works for your life. Think of it as your financial signature—the unique way you save, spend, and invest that feels authentic to who you are. Maybe you're the kind of person who thrives on a detailed spreadsheet, tracking every penny like it's a game. Or maybe you're more "vibes and vibes only," relying on automated systems to keep you in check while you focus on living your best life. Either way, the magic happens when you stop comparing your money moves to everyone else's and start trusting your own rhythm.

The truth is, financial freedom isn't just about having more money—it's about feeling empowered by the choices you make with it. It's the confidence to turn down plans that blow your budget without feeling guilty. It's the ease of knowing you can treat yourself because you've built a foundation where your savings goals are already handled. And it's the clarity that comes when your spending aligns with what actually matters to you—not what the world says should matter.

But here's where things get real: sustaining that energy for the long haul means turning your short-term wins into lifelong habits. It's easy to feel financially fierce when you're on a budgeting high or after a particularly successful savings streak. The real power comes from keeping that energy when life gets messy—because it will. Unexpected expenses pop up. Social pressures don't disappear. And the temptation to fall back into mindless spending never fully goes away. What changes is your ability to pause, check in with yourself, and stay committed to the bigger picture.

A huge part of owning your financial era is embracing flexibility without losing focus. Maybe there's a season where you're aggressively saving for a big goal—like moving to a new city or taking a once-in-a-lifetime trip. Then, there might be moments when you ease up and let yourself indulge more because your foundations are solid. Both approaches are valid. The key is knowing when to push and when to let go without spiraling into the all-or-nothing mindset. Financial wellness isn't a straight line—it's a dance between discipline and joy.

And don't underestimate the power of financial identity. Who you believe yourself to be with money shapes how you interact with it. If you see yourself as "bad with money" or someone who's constantly playing catch-up, you'll keep reinforcing those patterns—even when you're fully capable of breaking them. Shifting that narrative means embodying the version of you who is already thriving. Picture your future self—the one who's got her finances on lock, who saves effortlessly while still enjoying life, who moves through the world with confidence because she knows she's got herself covered. Now, start making decisions as her.

Owning your financial era also means knowing when to recalibrate. Your goals, desires, and lifestyle will evolve—and your money habits should evolve with them. What worked when you were in survival mode might feel restrictive when you're stepping into a phase of abundance. Check in with yourself regularly. Are your financial habits supporting the life you want right now? Are you saving for things that still light you up, or are you holding onto goals that no longer fit? The power lies in knowing you can always shift gears.

At the heart of it all, staying financially fierce for the long haul is about blending awareness with intention. It's not about never spending—it's about spending with clarity. It's not about hoarding every penny—it's about saving for the life you actually want. And it's definitely not about being perfect—it's about being present and proactive in your relationship with money.

Your financial era isn't a destination—it's an energy. It's the moment you realize you're the main character in your money story, and you get to decide how that story unfolds. Whether you're just beginning to reclaim control or already living your best financially empowered life, one thing's for sure: this era? It's yours—and you're owning every part of it.